For King and Country

BOOK ONE: THE CALLING

K.E. GUZMAN

Print ISBN: 979-8-88589-153-0

e-Book ISBN: 979-8-88589-154-7

Contents

 1. July 27th, 1914   1
 2. August 4th-7th, 1914   19
 3. August 8th-31st, 1914   35
 4. September 3rd-12th, 1914   51
 5. October 16th-18th, 1914   65
 6. October 19th-20th, 1914   77
 7. November 21st-30th, 1914   91
 8. December 24th-25th, 1914   103
 9. January 1st-8th, 1915   111
10. March 10th, 1915   117
11. March 11th, 1915   123
12. March 12th, 1915   135
13. March 13th, 1915   149
14. March 14th, 1915   163
15. April 15th-May 2nd, 1915   175

CHAPTER 1

July 27th, 1914

The air felt thicker that day as Gale Arlington Jr. and Charles Dunford made their way to the Elephant and Castle pub. It was hot and cloudy, making the atmosphere sticky with the unpleasant summer humidity that was common for the South of England, especially in London where the Thames, congested by steamers of all sizes, emitted a pungent sort of mist that only added to the dank, heavy feeling that surrounded Gale and Charles. The two were running late. That was normal for them, of course. Gale had a tendency to forget his pocket watch, and Charles never had the need to be aware of time—he was well off enough that the passing of minutes to hours meant very little, and he didn't mind who knew it.

"They said it'd be right around the corner from the station," Gale said as he scanned the buildings. He looked for the dark exterior that set most neighborhood pubs out from the rest of the gray buildings that reached into the smog-and-cloud filled sky. It was threatening to rain and had been all day. Gale secretly hoped it would get it over with already so maybe there could be some relief of the humidity. Summer in the city always made him feel like every speck of dirt and cloud of smog would be stuck to him by the end of the day. But it wasn't anything that a pint of beer couldn't solve. If his father knew he and Charles were going to a pub, even one in Kensington, he'd have a lot to answer for. Usually the two of them would go to the club, maybe have curry, play some billiards, and talk to their school friends. A perfectly respectable afternoon for two nineteen year olds, next in line for their families' wealth and business. But, if Gale was being honest, he'd have to say that he preferred the company of the McGuinness brothers at a simple pub. The air in the room wasn't weighed down by privileged judgment and expectation.

Charles looked around; he was taller than Gale was and could therefore look over the crowd of bustling Londoners. Neither young man fit in with the typical drab city look that most of the men and women that were on the street carried. Instead of brown or gray suits and trousers, they were in lighter blue and cream-colored clothes, unworried about getting their clothes dirtied; after all, when they returned to school, a maid would clean them. Besides, it was still hot and muggy, the idea of wearing thick wool clothes that day seemed unbearable. Sweat was already sticking Gale's collar to the back of his neck. He shrugged his shoulders to dislodge it as he and Charles continued to look on.

"Was it Rory?" Charles asked.

"Yes, yes it was," Gale replied.

"Well that's the problem. Rory barely knows his right from his left on good days, let alone when a pub is involved," Charles laughed.

"The man only knows his directions when it comes to going to the pub," Gale laughed back, then a smile crossed his face. "See, it's there!" Gale pointed to a dark-looking building. It was a black-painted, wood-ensconced pub. The words "Elephant and Castle" were painted in gold paint, the letters were slightly worn, making it hard to read what they said from the street. "Rory always knows what he's talking about." Gale strutted off across the street, deftly dodging the milieu of carts and buggies that were clogging up the streets. Charles quickly followed, just managing to suppress an amused eye roll.

The two walked into the pub, blinking to let their eyes adjust to the dim light provided from the few yellow glass gas lamps from the walls. They looked around to find the McGuinness boys—they were a pretty distinct group of brothers. Arthur, the oldest at 23, was as tall as he was strong. Even sitting, he managed to dwarf most at the table with him, except for Charles, who just barely matched him for height. Arthur also had broad shoulders from rowing, which he had somehow managed to maintain after he graduated from university and began to work as a clerk. Gale had always assumed he did it by helping the pretty baker's daughter bring sacks of flour into the bakery that was right next to the bank he worked at. But Gale would never ask, for Arthur would turn about a thousand different shades of red and keel over before admitting he fancied her.

Finn, the middle brother of 21, was just barely above average height and was the definition of wiry. He hunched his shoulders in to make himself seem even smaller than he was. Gale always thought that it was so he could fade into the background and read in peace. He was in his last year of university, taking an accelerated course of study, it was often said that he was too smart and observant for his own good. He'd spend hours in the library trying to solve the mysteries of the world even if that meant his classwork was left undone. Luckily, he didn't need to study too long to get the highest marks in the courses. Sometimes he misread situations, or his curiosity would get the better of him and he'd ask questions he shouldn't or make connections that others would miss. Finn was passionate about linguistics and philosophy; get a drink in him and you'd be stuck listening to him wax poetic about the societal implications of the existence of the Rosetta Stone. He'd paid many visits to it at the British Museum. Despite his love of language and philosophy, like his older brother, he decided to focus his studies on accounting and business. It was practical and made sense if he wanted to secure a real future. Gale thought it was kind of sad, but he couldn't talk. After all, he was studying law to join his father's firm.

The youngest of the McGuinnesses was Rory. He was the same age as Gale and Charles. He was Gale's height and had a mischievous smile that made you worry about what he was going to say next. Although he managed to never say the thing you worried about, it was as if he knew exactly what needed to be said at any given moment. He wasn't manipulative, instead, he had an understanding of how to put anyone at ease with a couple of sentences. He had managed to get a scholarship based on his essays about the toiling of the working class. They were a bit subversive for Oxford but their quality was apparently so astonishing the board had to let him in. He understood the power of words and how they could impact others. Gale was certain that he was either going to become a politician or the best salesman in the world. Either way, Gale wasn't sure which would be better (or worse, the voice at the back of his mind supplied) for the world. Thinking about it, all of the McGuinnesses had something that was special about them, Arthur was a first-class rower, Finn was so intelligent that it was scary, and Rory had a charisma that could get him into any room. That's how they managed to get into Oxford. Their family wasn't the most ... privileged. Their father was a factory foreman, and their mother was a seamstress. They were better off than many but still struggled to afford the uniforms and scholarly gowns required to be worn on campus. The three of them worked twice as hard as Gale and Charles, and the two privileged boys had no qualms about that.

"Oi! Over here!"

Gale turned his head and saw Rory waving his hand excitedly. They had managed to secure a booth that would be just big enough for Gale and Charles to squeeze into. That, or one of them was going to have to grab a chair from one of the tables. Charles had hot-footed it to the open seat next to Arthur. Gale looked at the other booth, but neither Finn nor Rory looked like they were going to budge over. Stealing a chair it was then. Gale quickly grabbed one of the chairs and lifted it up. Last time he had dragged the chair over, it had squealed loudly against the wooden floor. He had gotten an earful from the barmaid, Ida, and he did not want to repeat that. The woman was a battle-ax, far too formidable to upset again.

Putting the chair down as quietly as he could manage to avoid her wrath, Gale sat down. Before he could even say hello, Rory was sliding a pint of amber ale toward him. He took a drink and listened as Charles began to regale the McGuinnesses about their adventure on the Tube.

"It was packed, why were there so many people? The work day isn't even over, yet. A woman had a thermos filled with soup."

"Chicken soup," Gale added.

"Yes, chicken soup, the smell filled the entire train car. It was disgusting," Charles said.

"It *is* the lunch hour," Arthur murmured.

"Right, well, still," Charles replied, "I could have forgiven the soup. But then, the car jerked, and the woman lost her grip of the thermos, and it spilled. Everywhere! It ran down the aisle. I'm pretty sure that it stained my trousers. Do you know how sickening the smell of soup and tobacco smoke is? That's what the car smelled like. For six stops. Six of them! We're taking a cab, I am not sorry, it's just not worth it."

Finn snickered from behind his book, and Rory rolled his eyes.

"Didn't know you were such a girl about these things. Who knew soup is all it would take to bring down one of the nations top swimmers."

"Ooh, bugger off. It was bloody disgusting, and I don't mind saying. I'm sure the noodles or whatever she had in there are now permanently part of the train car's floor," Charles continued.

"I had no idea it had bothered you that much. We could have just gone into another car."

"And admit defeat? I think not!" Charles said. His tone was sincere, but the quirk at the side of his mouth and the glint in his eyes made it clear he was joking.

"Next time, I'll be sure to delay meeting up until after work. I'd love to see you in the tube at its most busy," Arthur added, speaking up a bit. He elbowed Charles, and pushed the younger man's pint closer. "Take a drink to get rid of the edge."

Charles didn't argue back. Instead, he took a long drink.

"Down in one?" Gale asked. He smiled, knowing that Charles was almost physically incapable of backing down from a challenge like that.

Charles groaned, but continued to tip the pint back. His Adam's apple bobbed as he drank the ale, the foam leaving a trail on the inside of the glass as he drained the beer. The rest of the boys watched him in silence as he finished off the pint. It wasn't much of a struggle. Over the last couple of years they had all gotten used to knocking a pint back with little thought. Charles put the pint on the table with a satisfying clink. "Happy?" Charles asked and cleared his throat, doing little to suppress the belch that was coming up from draining the ale so quickly.

"Almost," Gale said, laughing. "Do it five more times and I will be."

Instead of responding, Charles rolled his eyes.

"So, what did you want to talk about?" Finn asked, looking at Gale.

"Right, well, I thought we could all go down to the country for the rest of the day. School's off. And you have the rest of the day off, right, Arthur?" Gale asked.

"What makes you think I want to spend the day off with you lot?" Arthur asked.

"Oh, quite right," Rory laughed, "don't let us interrupt your hopeless staring at Sandra."

Arthur turned bright red. "I-I have other things of importance to do, I'll have you all know."

"Sure you do. Like carrying sacks of flour for Sandra, and daydreaming about Sandra, and following Sandra. Right?" Rory continued.

"That is not true. At least I have a girl. What about you? Huh?"

"This isn't about us," Charles said, "you're the one that doesn't want to go out to the country. We can take my car and everything, but you have more important things ... like what, writing poetry for Sandra?"

"Sighing after her, perhaps?" Finn chimed in.

Arthur looked at Gale with a pleading look.

"Don't look at me, they're making some pretty fair observations, after all, look at your shoulders. They don't get that way from clerking all day. That's for sure."

"You are all the worst. I need better friends."

"Hey, you're related to some of us. Trapped forever," Rory replied. He reached over the table and punched his brother on the shoulder.

"Watch it," Arthur warned.

Rory sat back down, hands out in surrender. "Okay, okay, I'll knock it off."

"Good. Now, you said you had your car? Why did you bother with the Tube?"

"I'm not driving it through half of London. It's in Knightsbridge, thank you very much."

"So you have to go back on the Tube then?" Finn asked. "Won't the soup bother you?" His voice and face were innocent. He meant the question sincerely.

"I think I'll be fine."

"Yeah, hopefully it won't be the same train on the way up again. And Charles was right, it did make the whole car smell sick. Pretty unideal," Gale said. "Right, well, finish your drinks, lads, and let's head out."

"Way ahead of you," Charles laughed. The rest of them knocked back their pints and left, waving at Ida behind the bar.

The group made their way to Knightsbridge and finally reached where Charles had left his Crossley 20/25 HP Tourer. It was painted a light teal color that was gleaming in the limited sun rays that broke through the cloud layer. The group just managed to pile into the car. It was a tight fit in the back, the leather-covered bench had barely enough room for Gale, Rory, and Finn to sit. Arthur pushed the rest of them—apart from Charles, who was driving—to the back seats.

"I'm a head taller than the rest of you, minimum, so no way am I sitting back there," he said. Gale didn't bother to argue. After all, it wasn't like he could shoulder his way in front of Arthur. It was going to be a very long drive from the way the three in the back were pressed shoulder to shoulder. Gale brought his elbows in, trying to hunch over like Finn habitually did, but couldn't quite manage it. Finn was in the middle, book already out on his lap. It was written in German, a language that Gale was, and this is true, hopeless at. Rory shifted his position over and over again, unable to find a comfortable position. Gale doubted he would, no matter how long he tried. Eventually, Rory slid down the seat and brought his leg up and was about to put it over the counsel of the car when Arthur turned around and glared at him. "Don't even think about it."

Without saying a word, Rory slowly brought his foot back down and sat up straight, pushing him, Finn, and Gale closer together.

It was going to be a very long drive indeed, Gale thought.

Charles stood in front of the car and began to crank the engine to life. It didn't take long when the automobile began to purr and growl, the power of the engine gently shaking the steel body of the vehicle. Charles jogged into the driver's seat, adjusted his leather gloves, and put the car into gear.

He deftly maneuvered the car into the streets of London and navigated the car through the winding roads, around pedestrians and horses. It was a marvel to look at the London buildings flying by them as the wheels spun. They got smaller and smaller and further apart. Gray faded into the greens and browns as the countryside started to pop up. Gale's grandfather's small estate was between London and Oxford. The roads quickly became less defined and unpaved the further into the countryside they went.

Finally, they reached the small country house that Gale's grandfather, John, lived in. There were enough rooms to host all the boys comfortably, and it was far less stuffy and formal than Charles's family's country manor. The house was made of red brick and bright trim. It was an old farmhouse that had been expanded during the 1860s by Gale's great grandfather.

Charles turned up the familiar drive and parked the Crossley, then took the key out of the ignition. Before the engine stopped running, Gale had already opened the back seat door and tumbled out, grateful to be able to immediately stretch his legs. Gale watched his friends climb out of the car. Charles, leaning back, popped his back. Rory tripped out of the car and fell flat on his face.

"That's what happens when you spend all day on your arse, Rory," Arthur laughed, staying in place while Rory started to get up.

"Not all of us are defined by sports," Rory grumbled in response, getting up and dusting off his trousers.

Finn tucked his book under his arm and, after looking Rory up and down, picked some invisible dirt off his younger brother's shoulder.

"I hope Mrs. Carson has some of those Scotch eggs," Charles commented. Gale hoped so too. Mrs. Carson was the housekeeper that did all the cooking and cleaning for his grandfather. She had taken on more hours since his grandmother had passed, and her Scotch eggs were famous. Gale made a point of eating as many as he could before he headed back to school. He was certain that Mrs. Carson made a point to make sure there was enough to satisfy the craving.

As Gale watched his friends make their way up to the house, Gale felt the thickness of the air grow and a heavy weight in his stomach build. He knew he was going to ask a lot of them in a few hours. But he wouldn't be able to live with himself otherwise. He took a deep breath and walked up the drive, jogging a little to catch up with the rest of them. They finally made it to the front door and just as he was going to push open the door, it opened, revealing Gale's father, waiting for them. He was in his forties, lines clear on his face. He looked like an older version of Gale, his reddish-blond hair just starting to gray. The set of his mouth was grim, and his blue eyes were surrounded by deep-set lines.

"That automobile of yours is so loud, the neighbor's sheep have already made a run for it," he said, looking at Charles.

"Sorry, Mr. Arlington," Charles said, head bowed just enough to show he was actually sorry.

Gale Sr. laughed and clapped Charles on the shoulder, "I'm joking with you, Charlie, come on in, boys."

The group filled in. Gale looked around, admiring the old rug and paintings that covered the floor and walls. It was a warm home, even though it was filled with the trappings of a far more formal one. Perhaps it was the smell of the pipe tobacco his grandfather habitually smoked. Or maybe it was the constant smell of cooking wafting up from the kitchen.

"Hello, Dad," Gale said, walking next to his father.

"Gale, how are your studies?" Gale Sr. always jumped right to business, wanting to make sure his son was doing him proud before returning to the kindly father Gale grew up around.

"Good, Latin is, well, it's Latin," Gale shrugged. There was no point in lying to him—his marks were slipping, and even though he asked Finn to help him, they were not making the progress he wanted.

"I never saw the point in studying Latin, is everything else good?"

"Yes, Father. Thank you for asking."

"Alright, I'm done interrogating," Gale Sr said. He clapped Gale's shoulder and guided him into the parlor.

Mrs. Carson was setting out a spread of small sandwiches and tea on the table. While her green eyes were still bright, there was a bit more gray in her brown hair since last time they all met. She smiled as everyone filed into the room. "If you need anything else, don't hesitate to shout." With that she left. Mrs. Carson wasn't one to linger, but sometimes Gale wished that she would. She was a friendly presence that always set him at ease.

"How's Mum?" Gale asked, looking at his father.

"She's well, you know how it is, managing the house. If she had it her way, she'd also be managing the neighbor's house," Gale Sr. laughed.

"Well, she does know the proper way to do things," Gale joked. By the time he and his father had finished their exchange, the rest of the group was sitting down and helping themselves to cups of tea. Charles lounged in an armchair, too familiar with the Arlington patriarch's house to bother with formalities. Arthur, Rory, and Finn were squeezed together on the cane sofa. There was another armchair and a loveseat left. Gale let his father take the armchair, and he resigned himself to the loveseat. He tried not to grimace as he sat down, the bench of the seat always felt like it was going to tip him forward. His grandfather had laughed when he had complained about it. "That's the point! Guests won't overstay their welcome if they're uncomfortable," he had said.

Just as Gale was about to ask if his grandfather would be joining them, the man appeared in the doorway. He was older, in his eighties. His red hair faded into mostly white after years of the stress of life weighing on him. Lines carved through his face, crow's feet and crinkles that told a story of a well-worn life. His eyes were the same blue that Gale and his father had, a deep-searing color that mimicked the Atlantic. But his visage held a degree of wisdom both his son and grandson lacked. Although if you were to peer into Gale Sr.'s eyes, you might see carefully concealed hints of the same hard-won wisdom.

"I thought I heard the circus was in town!" he said, half laughing. All Arlingtons had a friendly sort of humor that made you want to sit down and share a few drinks with them, maybe smoke a cigar or two.

The group greeted John warmly with a series of "Hullo John," and "Nice to see you"s. Gale Sr. got up and left the armchair. He strode over to the other armchair that Charles was occupying. Gale watched as his father simply raised his eyebrow at the teen, and Charles was up like a shot. Charles looked over at Gale. Gale looked back.

"I've heard the floor is perfectly suitable for sitting for tea," Gale said, not wanting to move and make the loveseat even more uncomfortable.

"Thankfully, I won't have to confirm the rumor of its comfort. There's a place right next to you," Charles replied.

"Don't—" Gale started. But, without letting his friend finish the sentence, Charles squeezed into the loveseat next to Gale. The loveseat itself creaked under the weight of the two of them. Both Gale and Charles gave each other a look that said: "If you break this chair, I swear to all that is holy ...".

"What has brought you all up from London to darken my doorstep, lads?" John asked.

"I invited them down, Dad," Gale Sr. said, "because there are some things I think we should all be talking about," he added.

"Ah yes, the whole Serbian mess, isn't it?" That was a typical example of an understatement that John Arlington was prone to making.

"The archduke's assassination?" Finn asked, trying to get some clarity.

"That is it, exactly." Any of the comfort and familiarity seemed to be sucked out of the room. Silence descended. It was clear that everyone had an inkling about what was about to happen.

"I think we should enlist," Gale said, shattering the silence.

"There's no war for us to enlist in," Arthur protested.

"Yet," Gale Sr. replied. "There is no war, yet. It's only a matter of time."

"But we don't know that, not for sure." This time it was Charles who spoke up.

"Germany is already involved, so is Austria, and Russia. It's only a matter of time, innit?" Finn said the question at the end of the sentence as just a formality.

"That's what I was thinking," Gale said, "*The Times* can say whatever they'd like, but ... let's be honest, the Kaiser is spoiling for a fight, and we aren't going to take that lying down, now, are we?" Gale proclaimed, his voice becoming more impassioned as he spoke. The more he thought about what it would mean for Britain to stay out of the war. To avoid the fight. Let alone what it would be like for him to sit it out. It was unthinkable. "I'm going to volunteer. It's the best bet, I think."

"Better to volunteer now than wait it out," Gale Sr. added. "The longer a war drags on the more desperate everything gets. You want to do your duty early and have a chance to rise through the ranks."

"Aye, this whole thing won't last, and if and when we get into this whole war, it'll be over in a few months. Home by Christmas, I say," John said. "Those Huns don't know what will hit 'em!"

Gale nodded. "If we want a chance to fight for the crown, it's now or never." His tone was authoritative, excitement building in him.

"Say, you two have fought in a war, haven't you?" Rory asked, looking between Gale Sr. and John.

"Yes, we have. I was in the Boer War," Gale Sr. said. "It was a mess, a lot of good men sacrificed a lot for the empire. We can't let their lives go to waste now." Rory, Finn, Arthur, and Charles gave each other dubious looks. Gale looked at them with a raised eyebrow. Why were they doubting? They'd get a chance to serve, get recognized for it. Being a war hero was nothing to sniff at. If nothing else, it'd give the McGuinnesses a chance to climb up the social ladder in a way that they wouldn't be allowed to without a war. Everyone would benefit.

"What's the hesitation? I don't get it. Are you going to be cowards, or are you going to be proud Britons? Give 'em what for!" Gale added, his frustration getting the better of him.

"I ... think it's a lot to consider," Charles answered diplomatically.

Gale swiveled himself around so he was facing Charles directly on the loveseat. They were even closer than Gale had realized. "What is there to consider?"

"What isn't there to consider?" Gale Sr. intervened before the two could begin to squabble, or worse, fight and break the creaking loveseat. "You need to know what you're getting into. Even a quick skirmish is nothing to scoff at.

Gale started to protest when John stood up, effectively silencing the room again.

"Your father's right, so you better listen up. It takes a lot to be a good soldier."

"Like what?" Finn asked.

"That's the rub, all wars are a bit different, but ... let me tell you what I know." John started to head over to the hearth. Just above the hearth, mounted on the wall, was a saber. It looked deadly, even as it was on display. The curved blade was polished, reflecting the pale sunlight, streaming in from the windows. The hilt was made up of a brass guard that wrapped around the tang to protect the hand. It was beautiful in a way that promised it had cut through flesh and drawn blood. He took it off the wall and brandished it with a practiced ease.

"I was in the cavalry," John started. "I had an affinity for riding horseback, and my father had pushed me into equestrian and fencing. He always wanted me to be a classic gentleman, just like him. Too bad

I never got a hang of the etiquette, eh?" He swung the saber back and forth. Letting the boys gawk at it. Gale Sr. simply took another sip of his tea, unbothered by the display. He had seen it before, heard the speech, it was nothing new to him. After all, he had seen war too.

"I fought in the Crimean War, in the 13th Light Dragoons." As John began to reminisce, he let himself lean more heavily on his cane, allowing him to gaze at the saber that sat comfortably in the palm of his right hand. His thumb ran over the scratches that covered the hilt, indicating just how much it had been used. "I nearly lost my life, more than once. If it weren't for the boys around me, I damn well would have been dead. The battle that really stuck with me. The one I think about when I close my eyes, or on those cold nights when my wound has decided to rear its ugly head," John continued, referring to the old injury to his left leg. "It was what would become known as the Battle of Balaclava, a real sight to behold. It was going to be a big fight, we all knew it. The night before I made sure to sharpen the blade of this saber. I had adjusted my pistol holster over and over again, making sure it was in the exact right place for me to pull the gun out without a delay. I instructed the men in my battalion to do the same; I didn't want a single man under my command to be underprepared, they needed to come back alive. My commanding officer was Lieutenant General James Brudenell. He was on horseback with the rest of us, at the front of the line. He had more balls than all of you lot combined. And was willing to put himself with the men he commanded, instead of hiding away in a tent behind the battlelines. They don't make them like that anymore, I'll tell you now."

"Hey, now, I don't think that's quite true," Gale Sr. protested. "My sergeant was like that, too. Put himself in the line of the guerillas down in South Africa—"

"Ah, it's just not the same," John replied, cutting Gale Sr. off. "Where was I? Oh, I know. I was scared as hell, all of us were. But then, he was there, in front of us. His horse was a bright white, standing out against the dirt and trees of the forest we were using as a base. He gave this ... empowering speech of valor and honor of man and then ... ordered us to charge. I looked to my left and right, and watched my friends press on. I urged my horse forward, into a steady gallop. We charged the Russian guns, but something was off. I couldn't tell you what, but I knew something was wrong. When you become a soldier you start to pick up on those things and you get a sixth sense for it. I didn't want to be right. The Russians weren't supposed to be ready for us. But we had barely made it to the ridge when we were shot at. Over and over again. My friends were dropping like flies. Smoke was everywhere; I could barely see; my eyes were burning. But I heard screaming. I continued forward and made it to the battery. My saber drawn, I slashed through tens of faceless men. There was so much screaming." John's eyes gained a faraway look. Gale wondered if he could still smell the smoke and feel the blood on his hands.

"I ... I turned around to help out my boys and my horse, Bosco, was shot down right from under me. I tried to get out of the way, but my leg got crushed under him. Some stray shrapnel cut into my thigh. I couldn't let it slow me down. I managed to drag myself out from under him, and I ran. My sergeant at the time was still on his horse, and I tried to call out to him, get new orders, but he didn't hear me. Or so I thought. But then he fell off his horse and I saw his face had been shot clean off ... horrid sight. I saw the Russians advancing and cut across the battlefields looking for my friends, or any one I recognized really. Finally, I found my Buddy, Hughes. He was completely pinned by his horse. It had rolled over him, and it was a miracle he was alive. I could just push through the fray, slicing through the enemy, and when I reached him and pulled him out from under the horse, the Russians were firing again. My saber wasn't enough, and I had to draw my pistol and start to return fire. Then, after what felt like hours of Hughes and I shooting and dodging bullets, the battle ended. Just like that. Too quick. It felt ... empty. I expected some grand and noble ending, like in the books. But war isn't like that. Battles aren't like that. At some point they're just over with. Then you're left with the death and rot that blankets the torn-up earth. There was no difference between the Englishmen, Turks, French, or Russians. All bodies look the same when they're dead, like a husk ..."

John began to trail off. Gale thought he was done, but the older man cleared his throat.

"That's how I got my Victorian Cross, you know," he said, looking at his grandson.

"Did you have any regrets, Mr. Arlington?" Arthur asked, looking like he was completely entranced by the story.

"I've told you before, Arthur, call me John. Mr. Arlington is far, far too formal for me," John said. He relaxed his grip on the saber, letting it hang vertically from his grasp. "I wish ... I had really cherished the men that surrounded me more. That I had spent more time with my friends and loved ones. You don't realize how much you rely on your friends until one day they aren't there. Friendships between men, the teams of soldiers, that's what win wars. I pray that you don't face what I did. But if you do, you all will have each other's backs."

A heaviness took over the air again. The silence was an oppressive feeling. His grandfather's tale was almost enough to make Gale want to back away from volunteering.

"Well, that's a delightful story to hear before we enlist," Rory piped up, shattering the silence.

"We still haven't decided that," Charles protested.

"You and I both know that if Gale signs up, we'll all follow," Rory shot back.

Charles sighed, looking like he was caught between resignation and annoyance. "You're right, but I won't thank you for saying that."

"It'll be an adventure! Besides, we won't be fighting the Russians this time. Just good old Jerry and his pals. Nothing we Englishmen can't take, right?" Gale said, trying to bring up the mood. "And, like Grandpa said, we'll all have each other's backs. We'll keep each other alive, fight, and come back just in time for Christmas dinner. C'mon, this could be the only chance we get, do you really want to be the only men in Britain to stay home for this?" Gale pressed, looking around the room.

"I'm always up for a good adventure," Rory said eagerly.

"I can't let my brother go alone; Mum'll box my ears," Arthur added.

"It'll be a good chance to practice my French and German," Finn said, quietly.

Gale turned to Charles, he was the only one who hadn't said anything yet. His face was twisted up in annoyance. "Well?" Gale asked, pushing him like it was another challenge.

"Oh, alright, let's do it," Charles said.

Gale let out a whoop and jumped up to a standing position.

"Good, that's the right choice, my boys," John said. He held out the saber. Gale walked over to it and put his hand over his grandpa's. Then, he was joined by Rory. Then Arthur. Followed by Finn and Gale Sr. And finally, Charles.

Gale looked around the circle of his friends, his father, and grandfather. "For King and Country," Gale prompted.

"For King and Country!" the rest of them cheered.

CHAPTER 2

August 4th–7th, 1914

Gale was right. Within a week, Germany invaded Belgium, and England declared war. There was no mincing of words, no more ifs or buts—it was going to happen. It was time for them to put their money where their mouths were and to enlist. Gale and the other lads stood in line. It was the first day the War Office in central London was open. The line stretched around the block and then some. Gale was surprised that there were so many ready and willing to join up. But, then again, who wouldn't have a chance to fight, to stop the Germans from expanding their empire. To stop their encroachment on the British Empire. It left a bad taste in Gale's mouth to think about the entire idea. The world speaking, what, German? No, thank you.

"How much bloody longer will this line take?" Rory groaned. "My feet are getting tired," he added, shifting his weight back and forth between each foot to prove the point.

"It's barely been twenty minutes, Rory," Arthur replied, sounding just like the older brother he was.

"Okay, why is everyone else here now, huh?"

"Because they're here to do the same thing we are, Rory," Gale said. "They all want a chance at Jerry too."

Rory let out an impatient huff and leaned to the side to get a look at the line that stretched out behind them. "Christ, look at those poor sods, gonna be here until the fat lady dies, let alone sings."

Gale and Charles shared a look between themselves and then one with Arthur, exasperation radiated off the three of them. Gale looked over to Finn, trying to see if he was as annoyed as the rest of them with Rory's complaints, but he was content, leaning against the wall, reading a small book titled *The Sentiment of Rationality*. He had tried to explain it to Gale, but it all sounded like a load of drivel to him.

"Well, we would have been there sooner if you hadn't wanted to stop at a pub," Charles commented, plucking off a piece of invisible dirt from his jacket.

"Nothing wrong with wanting some liquid courage to sign my life away," Rory said. "Besides, I heard they do physical drills. I wanna be limber before I have to run through calisthenics, thank you very much. Not all of us are athletes."

"You know, I wish that I had another round if I knew you were going to be complaining the entire time," Charles said.

"Don't be so rude," Rory replied.

"Lads, can we please just get along? The line is already moving forward. We'll be in the medical exams before you know it, a matter of minutes," Gale said confidently.

It did not turn out to be a matter of minutes as Gale had hoped, but rather, they stood in line for three hours. In the sweltering heat of the summer the wait felt much longer. Even Gale's spirits felt a little dampened by the time they made it through the door of the War Office. The lieutenants and captains managing the desks looked just as harried as he felt. Some were standing at attention, Gale wasn't sure if they were there to be models of whom the volunteers would become or if they were meant to feel imposing. Either way was effective for him. A man stood behind a wooden table that had clearly been placed in the foyer of the War Office that morning. It was covered with stacks of official-looking documents, pens, and clipboards. "Step forward please," the man behind the table said. Despite the pleasant request tacked on the end, it was clear it was an order from his tone.

The captain hadn't looked up, nor directed the order to anyone.

But Gale realized that he and Charles had been shuffled by the rest of the boys to the front. No one stepped forward and the captain looked up, staring straight ahead. Gale looked around and then pointed at himself as if to ask: Me? Looking at the uniform, the man had three Bath stars on his epaulets. A captain. The captain gave him a bored, slightly annoyed look.

"Yes, you, c'mon, hurry it up," he barked.

Gale quickly stepped up and was given a clipboard and pen. There was a blank enlistment form clipped in place. The captain looked at him expectantly. "Well," he said, "fill it out and give it back to me," he said, annoyance overtaking the boredom. Gale quickly looked down the form. It looked exactly how he expected it to. It asked for his name, date of birth, where he was from, it seemed to go on forever, and he suddenly became aware of just how much he would be signing away. But it would be worth it. He thought about his ideals, what it meant to be a part of keeping the Germans back and saving their allies in France and Belgium. He was an honorable man. He was going to become an honorable soldier. Gale shifted to the side to accommodate Charles as the Captain gave him another clipboard to fill out alongside Gale. The two of them scribbled away, signing their names to serve King and Country. Finally, he reached the last dotted line asking for his signature and the date. Without hesitating, Gale signed: *Gale Arlington II*, 4th August, 1914.

Clearing his throat, Gale got the attention of the captain and handed him back the clipboard. The captain scanned the form, checking to see if Gale had missed anything, but he nodded, appearing satisfied. The captain handed him a small card with a number and letter, 241A, written on it. "Come back with this card in three days' time on the 7th. You'll be given a medical exam and physical test. If you pass, you'll be given a uniform, and you'll be shipped out. Understand?"

Gale nodded and waited as Charles finished his form and handed it to the captain. He received the exact same orders as Gale and got a card that read 242A. The two of them exited, waving at their friends to signal they'd be waiting outside for them. All three of the McGuinness brothers were waiting, Arthur and Finn, patiently, Rory, tapping his foot like he had a meeting with the Archbishop of Canterbury in a quarter of an hour. When the two made it outside, they gave each other a look and burst out laughing. "Did you see Rory's face?" Gale managed to gasp out between laughs.

"He looked so mad!"

"I thought his head was going to pop off!"

The two managed to calm down enough and started to lean back against the wall of the war office building. There was still a line that reached around the block.

"Three days," Gale commented as he caught his breath.

"I don't even know what to do for three days," Charles replied.

"Visit family?" Gale suggested. He was looking up in the sky, his eyes and nose crinkled up as he gazed into the sunlight.

"Probably," Charles said. "Should say bye to Mum and Dad, or something."

"Did you even tell them you were enlisting?"

"I'm sure they've already guessed."

Gale sucked air through his teeth. He rocked back on his heels, then looked at Charles. "I'm sure they'd still want to be told," he said gently. Charles didn't have a bad relationship with his parents. It was just very impersonal. He was close to his nanny growing up, but the second he reached fifteen, she was relieved of her duties. Gale wasn't sure Charles ever got over it. She had moved away, and he never saw her again. Only when he was drunk would Charles admit that he missed the woman that really raised him.

"I'm going to see them, don't worry. Father dearest will be most proud of me, I'm sure," Charles' tone was cool, a warning for Gale to stop pushing.

"Well, after you do, you should come back to Grandad's. He'll be thrilled to see you before we ship out."

"If we ship out. We still have exams, you know."

"I know, I know. But I'm of sane mind and strong of body. You are too. We're going to ship out," Gale said. He had made up his mind. It was the right thing to do, and if he had to drag his friends with him kicking and screaming, he would.

Charles nodded. He pulled out an ornately decorated silver cigarette case and grabbed out two cigarettes. "Want one?" he asked.

"Sure." Gale reached out and plucked the cigarette from his friend's fingers. He reached into his pocket and pulled out a match. Dragged it against the brick wall, lighting it. He lit his cigarette then passed the still burning match to Charles. He took a drag, letting the heady scent of burning tobacco fill his nose. The smoke filled his lungs, giving a pleasant burning warmth in his chest. He exhaled and watched the gray smoke fade into the air.

The two leaned against the building in a comfortable silence. Gale was just about to ask what was taking the McGuinnesses so long but, before he could even start to form the words, Rory's voice cut through the sound of afternoon traffic.

"Christ, what was that guy's problem, huh?" Gale and Charles leaned over to give themselves a better look at the exit door of the War Office. Rory's face was red and splotchy—clearly he was boiling over and fed up from waiting around.

"He can still hear you, Rory," Finn said, following his younger brother out. Arthur was the last one to exit, he looked annoyed. Gale wasn't sure if he was annoyed at his brothers or the enlistment process.

"I don't care, you asked a simple question. He shouldn't get his knickers in a twist about it."

"Rory, I appreciate it, but it's fine," Finn said placatingly.

"Seriously, I bet he's got something to do with the regiment assignments. I don't want him to hate us, already," Arthur added. He squeezed the bridge of his nose, like he was trying to stop a headache that was well on the way to forming already.

"What happened?" Gale asked.

"I wanted to know what it meant by place of origin. That's all. I don't know where I was conceived, I wasn't exactly there for the process," Finn explained, a little embarrassed. "So, if not that, then did he mean where I was born? Which would be the hospital? Or the town? Or region? I just wanted to make sure I was filling the form out correctly."

"Yeah, 'cept the bugger thought he was being funny and took offense."

Gale nodded, that made a lot of sense to him. It was unfortunately a common experience. Finn would ask for clarity and—

"It's not like Finn was taking a piss," Arthur added, unknowingly finishing Gale's thought for him.

"I'm sorry that happened, Finn," Gale said sincerely. "You were just double checking."

"It was a lousy form anyway. I had the same questions," Charles added. The group all hummed in agreement.

Gale took another drag of his cigarette. "Right, well, three days?"

"Three days," Arthur echoed.

"I was thinking of inviting you all round mine the night before we go back. Pester my dad and grandad for any more advice. What do you think?" Gale asked.

"You know I'll be there," Charles said before taking a long drag of his cigarette.

The McGuinnesses looked back and forth between each other until Arthur looked at Gale. "Yeah, we'll be there too," Arthur said, clearly getting a consensus from the silent signals sent by his brothers.

"Great, sounds good. See you then," Gale said. The group parted ways. A wave of excitement and unease seemed to roll through the group and they left each other.

Gale had gone home to his father's house. He spent the two days he was there pestering his father and mother and debating what he needed to pack, if anything. How much would they let him bring along? He ended up just throwing together a satchel with his Dopp kit, a pack of playing cards, a couple extra socks, a change of clothes and a family portrait. It depicted him, his father, mother, and grandfather. It had been taken a year ago. As he looked at it, he was surprised at how austere they seemed in black and white. He traced his hand over the arc they formed. His grandad was sitting in an armchair, Gale Sr. behind him. Gale and his mother flanked them. John had his cane in front of him, his old hands crossed and draped over the handle. Gale and his father had the same stony face as John. It was unreadable and cold, as if they were daring anyone to say something disparaging about them. Only Gale's mother, Louisa, had a gentle look to her. She was warm and nurturing when she wasn't wrapped up in her volunteer work. He knew that she worked just as hard as his father to maintain their tenuous place among the upper class. As nouveau riche, they had to fight to be respectable, and part of that included her working day in and day out for ladies' societies and volunteering for charities.

Louisa had made a point to be home when Gale told her the news. Gale Sr. refused to tell her for him, saying that if he was going to go to war, he could man up enough to give the news to his mother. She hadn't reacted in the way he expected. She hadn't cheered with jubilation nor burst into tears, prematurely grieving him. Instead, she smiled and said she was proud of him. He wanted her to say more, but she didn't. Rather, every time he saw her she'd give him a gentle grin. Sometimes she'd straighten his tie or pick off invisible lint. Other times she'd brush his hair to the side. Little doting actions that she used to do all the time when he was little, but since he had grown up had long since stopped. That was almost more difficult to deal with than tears, especially when she reached up to ruffle his hair. Gale had been taller than her by the time he was twelve, but she still seemed like such a large, comforting presence when she walked into the room.

The day came for Gale to meet the boys at his grandfather's place. Louisa had made sure the cook had put out a massive spread for breakfast. At some point while he was reading the newspapers, she had snuck off. At the time he'd wondered where she was, but, when he and his father were driving through the countryside, he looked at the contents of his bag. Everything was refolded far more neatly than he could ever have done. On top of the contents sat a small note. All it said was: *Be safe, my sweet boy.* He wasn't sure what he thought of that. Gale wasn't the most sentimental of people, but she had always called him that as a child. He remembered hearing her say that any time he ventured out to play in the woods or the fields as a child. Or else when he and Charles were getting up to no good and she knew someone would box his ears by the end of the day. It made him feel small as he sat in the passenger seat, the rolling fields of the English countryside blazing past. He sighed and tucked the note to the very bottom of the bag and buckled its dark leather shut.

The drive wasn't that long between his father's and grandfather's homes. Both were big enough to be respectable. Gale Sr. still commuted to work in London, so it made sense to live closer to the city. As they pulled into the gravel road, Gale realized that it was going to be the last time he saw his John's stately home for a long time. *Or ever*, a small voice whispered in the back of his head. Gale shook off the doubt filling his head and hopped out of the car to join his father as they walked up the drive to see John.

That night the rest of the group had made their way to John's place. They were sitting down having dinner. Gale Sr. and John were trading war stories, making the boys laugh. Gale looked back and forth between Charles, Arthur, Finn, and Rory. A warmth filled his chest, he knew that he was going to have their backs and they were going to have his. Together, they would keep each other safe. The dinner was winding down, and they were all sipping brandy, too full to move from the table and go to the drawing room or parlor. But suddenly John stood up. For once he wasn't leaning on his cane. He stood up straight and cleared his throat. "I would like to say a prayer. I'm not the most faithful follower of Christ. But this is a prayer that helped me in Crimea. And I hope it will bring you the same comfort it brought me."

Gale nodded, wanting to hear the prayer too. If he was honest, God and religion were rarely on his mind. He hadn't been to church since Easter; he was seasonal Anglican at best. John cleared his throat again, disturbing the seemingly permanent phlegm that lingered in his throat as he got older. In the flickering of the gas lights and candles, he looked older, closer to his age of eighty-three, than he usually did. The lines on his face looked deeper, and there was a tiredness—or was it a weight on his shoulders—that Gale had never seen before. He was about to start the prayer, and Gale realized he didn't know what he should do. He glanced at his father, who helpfully lifted his hands that were folded together and made a show of bowing his head. Gale followed suit, and he could tell everyone else at the table followed him. They must have been just as clueless as he was. He knew Finn didn't believe in God. He spent way too much time reading philosophy books, or so he had said. Come to think about it, the only one he knew that went to church regularly was, surprisingly, Charles. But Gale knew Charles went for the sole reason of keeping his parents off his back.

"It goes like this," John said, pulling Gale from his thoughts. "Grant us, Lord, in all our duties thy help, in our perplexities thy counsel, in danger thy protection, and in sorrow thy peace; in the name of Jesus Christ, our Lord. Amen."

"Amen," Gale Sr. and Charles said, nearly automatically.

"Amen," the rest of them chimed in after a moment of hesitation, trying to keep up.

"Right, well, I just wanted to share that with you. It got me through a lot. I won't debate with any of you about God. But I wanted you to feel like you had something to help ground you the way it helped to ground me," John said. He sat back down in the chair. The heaviness resting on his shoulders seemed to be weighing his entire body now. He was staring at a candle, watching the flame dance from a draft that seemed to suddenly cut through the room. A shiver ran up Gale's spine. He wondered what his granddad was thinking about. What memories were running through his head in that moment to give him the faraway look to his gaze. Was he thinking about the battle he had gotten his leg wound from? Or another one?

When Gale turned to look at his dad, it became clear that he too was thinking about some battle in the Boer War. Gale wanted to ask them directly to share their thoughts. But from the set of their mouths and the sorrow creeping into their gaze, he knew better than to push.

The group retired for the evening not long after that. They had bid each other goodnight. All of them knew the next morning the boys were heading to the War Office and then from there, France. As

Gale laid in his bed, the window open to let the summer air into his room, giving it some sort of movement to get rid of the stale air, he looked back to the sky. The stars were out and twinkling down. He wondered if they could tell there was a war on? He realized that they had probably witnessed countless wars. Silent, inanimate sentries looking down and watching humanity. If they could speak, would they pass judgment on man? Gale eventually managed to fall asleep as he continued to mull through that very question.

———————

When Gale entered the War Office the next day, it looked the exact same. The same captain was standing behind the table and giving orders. Gale was at the front of the line, and this time he was ready to be addressed. The captain barely looked up when he did finally give an order to Gale. "Give your card to the doctor," the captain said and then pointed to a hallway that jutted out behind him and the same makeshift booth from when he had volunteered. He turned back to the line where the rest of the lads were waiting to be processed along-side Gale.

Gale took a deep breath, set his shoulders and began to walk down the hallway. Time seemed to slow with each step he took. Every foot-step seemed to echo loudly, radiating through his entire body. Gale became hyper aware of his breathing and heartbeat, blood rushing through his ears to the rhythmic thumping. Behind that door, Gale was going to meet a doctor. That doctor was the most serious obstacle between him and becoming the soldier he knew he was meant to be. He didn't believe that he had any sort of disability, defect, or impair-ment that would stop him. But as he reached the door that had a small handwritten sign that read "Knock, then wait," tacked to it, Gale began to worry that maybe there was some underlying illness that would be detected. As he listened to his own heartbeat, he couldn't help but wonder if he was hearing a faint murmur. His lungs were constricting, his breaths felt shallower than ever before, was that asthma? Or maybe his feet would be considered too flat. Or his eyesight was worse than he thought. Hundreds of possibilities ran through his head. The idea of being deemed unfit for the military made Gale feel sick to his stomach. Being deemed medically unfit would be the worst way to be turned away. Visions of being left behind at Oxford while his friends left to fight the good fight swirled through his mind. What would he even do if that happened?

How could he stay behind while others put their lives on the line? It would be unconscionable. As Gale raised his fist to knock on the oak door, he resolved to find a way to sneak on the boat before it shipped out to France or wherever it was heading. Charles would help him out, he knew it. He knocked three times and waited.

Just as Gale was about to knock again, a clipped voice rang out. "Enter!" Taking another deep breath to settle his nerves, Gale opened the door and stepped inside.

The exam room was small. It was clearly an office of some high-ranking official that had been seized and converted for the rush of enlistments. There was a large, dark-stained oak desk, a map of the empire, and a large bookshelf to the side. In addition to the office furniture, a sturdy-looking table that looked to be a little over six feet long sat between Gale and the doctor. The doctor looked like he had been standing in the stuffy room for hours adjusting his collar and white coat, ignoring Gale as he stepped into the room.

Gale waited for him to turn around and look at him, but the man just kept adjusting his tie. Gale cleared his throat, doing his best to get the attention of the doctor. "One moment," the doctor said. Then, with a final adjustment and defeated sigh, the doctor turned to Gale.

"No matter what I do, this damn coat and tie are going to suffocate me in the heat," he sighed. He picked up a clipboard that was on the desk. It looked like another long form. Gale briefly wondered if he was going to have to fill it out. "Now, I'll take that," the doctor said, pointing to the card that Gale still held between his index and middle finger. He had forgotten about it in the short walk between the foyer of the War Office and the exam room.

"Oh, right, of course, here you go, sir," Gale said, quickly handing the card over.

The doctor raised an eyebrow and plucked the card from Gale's grasp. "You're a talkative one, aren't you," he commented. Before Gale could even try to think of a response, he continued, "Now, hop up on the table." Gale did as he was told. "Remove your jacket and shirt. I'm going to listen to your breathing and heartbeat. Understand?"

Gale nodded. It sounded like a usual doctor's exam. He quickly removed his jacket and shirt, half folding them, half tossing them on the table beside him. The doctor pulled out a stethoscope and crossed behind him. With no warning, the doctor pressed the cold metal against his skin. Gale inhaled sharply, shocked at the chill against the stifling heat.

"Inhale," the doctor ordered.

Gale inhaled.

"Again."

Gale inhaled, again.

"Everything sounds clear to me." The doctor crossed around the table to face Gale directly.

With the same lack of warning, he pressed the stethoscope into his chest and listened to his heartbeat. The doctor hummed. "Are you nervous?" he asked.

"Uhhh ..."

"No need to lie to save face. Are you nervous?"

"I ... I guess," Gale replied as anxiety spiked through his system.

The doctor continued to press the stethoscope into his skin and looked at his watch. Gale sat in silence, desperately trying to slow his heartbeat. But the more he thought about slowing it, the faster it seemed to tick up. He could feel the rushing of his pulse. After fifteen seconds, the doctor sighed deeply and took off the stethoscope. He wrapped it over his neck and took a step back from Gale. The doctor looked him over with an assessing keen gaze. He then pointed to the wall across from Gale, where the nineteen year old saw a piece of paper with lines of random letters of various sizes. "Read the sixth line down for me?"

"E, D, F, C, Z, P," Gale recited with no trouble. As Gale read the line, he noticed the doctor begin to scribble notes onto the form on the clipboard. Anxiety roiled through his body, setting him on edge. He couldn't help but wonder what was being written about him.

"The last line?"

"Z, E, F, P ...T, E, C," Gale read, taking a moment to be sure the T was actually a T and not a P trying to trip him up.

"Good. What's your height?"

"Five foot nine."

"Good. Put your shirt back on." As Gale pulled his shirt on, the doctor gave him another assessing look. "Your heart rate was ... accelerated. But, you seem to be in good health otherwise. And as long as you swear to me you don't have any other underlying conditions, I'm going to say that you're nervous. Okay? You're nervous."

"Okay, uh, yeah, I swear, healthy as an ox."

The doctor looked satisfied with Gale's response. He clipped the card to the medical form and handed it to Gale. "Go through that door, take a right, and you'll find a sergeant with another group of prospects. Wait with them until you're given your next orders. Understand?"

Gale took the paper and nodded. "Yes, sir."

"Good, now, off you pop." Just as the doctor finished his sentence there was a knock at the door. "Go," he said, making a shooing motion. Gale hopped off the exam table, grabbed his jacket and went through the back door of the office the doctor had pointed to.

He followed the doctor's directions, turning right down a long hallway. Gale marveled at how large the War Office seemed. On the outside it seemed like it was just another neighborhood constabulary that had been co-opted by the military and retrofitted for enlistment. But it was sprawling and made Gale hyper aware of the scale of the enlistment program. How many men were they aiming to sign up? How many did they think they needed to win the war? How many were ... expendable?

Before he could let his mind drift any further, Gale heard a commanding voice echoing out through the halls. "Get in line, stand at attention!" That must be the sergeant, that or the man barking orders was doing his best to mimic one. Gale continued down the hallway, following the booming voice until he made his way into what looked like a large canteen made into a gym.

There were cricket goals on either side of the large room. On one side, there were two other men standing at a civilian's approximation of attention. Gale hoped that years with his father and grandfather made him ready to get the postures exactly correct. Gale got in line with the two others and stood at attention. The sergeant watched his every move with a hypercritical gaze as if he were looking for any reason to yell. Relief poured through his body as he seemed to pass muster.

Then soon after he got in line, Charles entered and did the same thing Gale did. The Arlington patriarchs had taught them well. The two didn't greet each other, but Gale was set at ease when his friend entered the room. Soon after, the McGuinness brothers filed in one by one. Each of them looked at the way Gale was standing and made their best attempt to match.

"Straighter!" the sergeant ordered, looking at Finn. It looked almost painful as Finn reluctantly stopped hunching and slouching and let himself stand at his full height, with his shoulders set. The sergeant looked appreciatively at Arthur as he strode in with the sort of confidence that comes from being a competitive athlete. Charles had entered similarly, but his relaxed attitude made it much less pronounced.

"Private!" The sergeant yelled. Out of a door on the perpendicular side from where Gale and the others were standing, a private quickly jogged out and met the sergeant. "Get the papers, then you are dismissed." The private mechanically did what he was ordered to do. It was clear he had been doing this all afternoon as well. His movements were practiced and exact. He didn't bother to really look at any of the men in the line up. Probably reassured that he needn't bother to memorize them, they were anonymous faces in a sea of volunteers.

The private left as quickly as he had arrived. The second the door shut, the sergeant began to pace back and forth down the line. "Push-ups, go!" The sergeant ordered.

Charles and Arthur were the first two to process the order. They quickly hit the deck and began doing pushups. Gale followed suit with only a hint of hesitation. Then Rory, the other men, and finally Finn. "Keep going; you stop when I say you stop!" It felt endless. Gale couldn't remember the last time he had done any push-ups. He glanced over to Finn out of the corner of his eye. The bookish man was struggling to keep up, his lag emphasized by his older brother's zeal. Shining black boots stepped in front of Gale's gaze. Gale looked up to see the sergeant staring down on him. "Don't look at him. Focus on yourself."

The sergeant put them through their paces, they did sit-ups, pull-ups, and running drills. Gale had a stitch in his side that felt like it was bigger than the entire continent of Europe. None of them were faring that well by the end. Charles and Arthur were still doing the best but in their wool and linen trousers they were constrained, sweat was being insulated against their skin. Everyone was miserable from the heat. "Stop!" The sergeant ordered. Everyone stopped, Gale was just barely able to keep standing upright. His heart was pounding. He had never considered himself out of shape. He was willing to admit he wasn't as fit as Charles, but he wasn't a collegiate athlete, after all. He didn't swim so his lungs didn't have the same huge capacity as his friend. But he never thought he was weak or lazy. But as he tried to keep up with the running and the pull-ups, he had found himself lagging behind. As Gale caught his breath, the door the private had entered opened again. The private stood by the door.

"Head on through, you've all passed," the sergeant said. "All you have next is to be fitted for your uniform and then you'll be on your way to Brighton, then Paris. Got it? Good. Dismissed."

Gale stood up straight and looked at Charles and quirked his eyebrow. He mouthed: "Told you we'd make it."

Charles rolled his eyes and mouthed back, "Sod off." Both snickered. Gale could feel a smile crossing his face.

Gale crossed over to Charles and the McGuinnesses. Finn was still panting hard but was slowly recovering. "This is what I get for quitting cricket," he grumbled.

"What?" Gale asked, "I didn't know you played cricket."

"Yeah, he's a damn good pitcher," Arthur said.

"Just wasn't my speed. Couldn't keep doing it if I wanted to study multiple things." Finn shrugged, just managing to get the words out between heaving breaths. "Running didn't used to be that hard," he added.

"You're complaining? I quit before I finished grade school. This is it, this is how I die," Rory complained. Gale laughed.

"I know how you feel. But, c'mon, let's go. The faster we get fitted, the better. I'm ready to get to France," Gale said. With that he started off to the door where the private was still standing. The other two men that had been put through their paces with them had already filed through. The private looked annoyed that he had to wait as long as he did.

"Sorry," Gale apologized as he walked through the door.

Behind him he heard Charles mutter. "It's like the git is excited to get shot at."

Gale turned around and rolled his eyes. "Just ready to get to the fight. I have a feeling that this is going to change everything."

CHAPTER 3
August 8th–31st, 1914

France is not what Gale had thought it would be. He had never been, but he'd read and heard stories of grand tours that detailed how life-changing a visit to the country could be, especially if one were to visit Paris. In Gale's opinion, there wasn't too big of a difference between the dirty Parisian streets and those in London. Only, somehow, the Parisians were even more snobbish than Londoners. How that was possible, Gale couldn't say. But as he and his friends walked the streets of Paris, he was comforted by the odd familiarity that came from walking down twisting city streets. One difference he did appreciate was the bakeries. He had taken a left when down a sunny street and had been hit with the smell of freshly baked bread. His stomach rumbled immediately, and Gale realized he hadn't really eaten in the last twenty-four hours. As proud as he was of his country, the food left something to be desired. Especially the military rations offered during the trip to France. Something about boiled pork and turnips just made him lose his appetite. But as Gale followed his nose, gesturing for the rest of the lads to follow him, he walked into a bakery that's scent had seemingly called to him.

As he walked in he saw two long banks of glass cases that held many different pastry delights, he was immediately drawn to the baguette sandwiches that were laid out pristinely in the right case.

Behind the case stood a bored looking older man that was surveying a group of lads dubiously. They were all dressed in their uniforms. They were telegraphing the reason they were there. Gale wondered what he made of them and the war that was simmering on the eastern border. The man looked at them and stepped up to the case, he gestured to the pastries in front of him, and then to the shelves filled with fresh loaves of bread.

"*Parlez-vous anglaise?*" Gale asked, he immediately knew his pronunciation was terrible. Language was not his strong suit. That was for sure. He turned to Finn, who was busy perusing the pastry case.

"*Non,*" the baker said, "*Je ne parle pas anglaise, monsieur.*" He looked annoyed to be asked, this must not be the first time his bakery had been inundated by a group of British soldiers. They were soldiers now, Gale thought. The word seemed to roll around his mind, the weight of the title settling over him during the past few days.

"Uh, Finn?" Gale said.

"Yeah?" Finn replied, looking up from the case.

"A little help, please?"

"Oh! Yes! Right away," Finn said excitedly as he walked up to the baker. "*Bonjour, monsieur,*" he started. Then he turned to the group. "What would you like?"

The group all told Finn their orders, and within a few minutes the lads were a few francs poorer but were rich in sandwiches. The group continued to wander the Paris streets. Technically, they were in search of a pub or bar they could spend some time in while they were waiting out their twenty-four-hour leave before they started training. But, instead they ended up walking around, exploring the city.

"I don't know how I'm going to survive if the food is always like what they gave us on the ship," Charles commented, taking a bite out of the baguette sandwich he had gotten, dijon, ham, and some sort of cheese none of them had heard of. It turned out the group all had the exact same taste because they all ended up ordering it.

"Wasn't too bad. I mean, food is food," Rory replied.

"Here we go," Gale whispered to Arthur and Finn. The three

snickered; as always, Rory decided to take the opposite opinion of Charles. No matter what. Rory claimed it was because he simply disagreed with every thought Charles ever had. Gale was certain it's because he just loved arguing and the sound of his own voice and telling Charles he was wrong. Regardless, Rory was lucky that Charles mostly thought it was funny. He, like Gale, didn't have any siblings, so it was a fun change of pace to have someone to squabble over petty arguments with.

"Yes, this is food," Charles agreed, lifting up his sandwich. "What we had on the ship was wet leather. You'd have to be a fool to think this," Charles again lifted and shook his sandwich to emphasize his statement, "and the rations are the same type of thing," Charles continued.

"Well, excuse me, Mr. Prim and Proper. Some of us didn't have access to fancy food growing up so we don't know better, right, Arthur?"

"No, don't drag me into this. I'm too busy eating," Arthur stated. He took a large bite of his sandwich to prove his point.

Gale couldn't help but laugh again at the antics of his friends. Everything felt right, the band of them together, days away from really becoming men and fighting in the name of the crown. He was ready to get basic training started. He was surprised when he was told they'd be heading straight to Paris from Brighton.

"Usually we'd train you down in Yorkshire, but we need boots on the ground sooner than later. You'll be learning as you go," one of the many captains that had processed them had said. Gale was amazed at just how disorganized the army felt as he was shuffled through war office after war office. By the time they had made it to Paris, Gale, Rory, Arthur, Finn, and Charles had been on a ship that left from Brighton, a train, and three trucks. It was a long journey that left them all a bit worse for wear. He caught his reflection in a shop window and saw just how harried and scruffy they all appeared. Their shoulders were all slumped, and it was clear that they hadn't really had a chance to rest much or wash up in the last day or so. He wondered if he'd get used to the feeling of exhaustion that inevitably came with being a soldier, or if it was going to take a long time for his body to adjust for it.

Finally, after another ten, maybe fifteen minutes, the group managed to find a small patio café that had plenty of other British soldiers. He saw a man that he recognized from the physical exams, sitting alone at one of the larger tables. He must have gotten there early. He was reading a copy of *The Times* and sipping a cup of tea. Gale made a beeline to him.

"Hello, I'm Gale. These are my friends Charles, Finn, Arthur, and Rory. Mind if we join you?" Before the man had a chance to say anything one way or another, Gale and the others were already pulling out chairs and sitting down.

"Oh, of course, please. I'm not using the whole table. I'm Thomas."

"Nice to properly meet you, Thomas," Gale said, reaching out his hand.

"I'm sorry?"

"You were in the same physical tests we were in back in London," Finn explained.

"Oh! Right, of course. Forgive me for not recognizing you all," Thomas said, quickly shaking Gale's hand and then the rest of them. "It's nice to see some familiar faces. I feel like I was the only one who didn't enlist with a group of friends to stick with."

"Well, as long as you are willing to keep sharing this table, you can stick with us," Gale offered. Thomas was quick to fit into the group. He was like a mix of Arthur and Finn, quiet but kindly.

"Why'd you join up?" Rory asked after about an hour of them getting to know each other. At this point they had finished two bottles of wine split between them. Never let it be said that Englishmen don't know how to pack away a drink.

"Yeah, it was a tough choice to volunteer, leaving my wife and son behind, but it's what's right. Better to stop the Jerries before they try to expand their reach even further. I sure am not going to let my son grow up speaking German," Thomas explained.

"Oh, you're married? How old are ya, then?" Arthur asked.

"Twenty-two."

"Ah, you're right between Arthur and Finn's age!" Rory proclaimed. He had had more than his fair share of wine; his cheeks were glowing a deep red color that matched the wine in the glass he was holding.

"Oh, good to know," Thomas said, at a loss of what else he could possibly say in response to that.

"Don't mind, Rory, he's more of a lightweight than he thinks," Charles laughed.

"Oi! That's not true!" Rory said, punctuating his sentence with a hiccup.

"I rest my case," Charles said, amusement clear in his tone.

"You're going to be in for a rough morning, huh?" Thomas said, giving Rory a sympathetic look.

The night continued on like that, the group laughing and bickering. Before they knew it, it was time to head back to the bunks. They found out that Thomas was assigned to the same building as them. "Makes sense," Thomas had drunkenly mumbled. "We all signed up at the same place and same time ... we're probably in the same unit."

As it turned out, when they were all assigned a truck to take to basic training, Thomas was right there with them, nursing the same headache the rest of them were. Gale looked around the truck. It seemed like they weren't the only ones dealing with the aftereffects of a night of drinking. The truck trundled along the unpaved roads taking them to God knows where. With each curve in the road or bump, Gale's stomach churned. He bowed his head, letting his body curl over; his hands dangling between his legs. Gale realized that he had never actually managed to get drunk on wine before. He only ever drank it during long, multiple course dinners his parents hosted every once in a while. He preferred a Scotch or simple beer. But, when in Rome ... But now, he had nothing but regrets. Something told him that he'd never be able to drink wine without thinking of this long drive ever again.

"You alright there, mate?" Gale looked up from staring down at the wooden floor of the truck and made eye contact with the soldier across from him. He looked concerned.

"Uh, yeah, just fine, thanks," Gale answered.

"You sure? You're looking a bit … green," he said. Then, before Gale could say anything, the soldier reached into his pocket and pulled out a small brown paper bag. "Here, take one." The soldier shook the bag.

"No, thanks, I'm fine, really."

"It's just a peppermint candy, seriously, take one. I'm trying to avoid getting sick on my new uniform, mate. So, please," The soldier insisted, holding the bag out to Gale. The last thing Gale wanted was a sweet, but if it got the soldier to leave him to his self-inflicted misery … He plucked a red-and-white striped candy and popped it into his mouth. The taste of peppermint took over his senses, and he felt his nausea fade just a bit.

"There, now you're looking a little less awful," the soldier said. Then after a moment, he held out his hand. "I'm Barry, Barry Fritz." Gale smiled and shook his hand.

"Gale Arlington Jr."

"Oh, you're a junior, huh? What does Gale Sr. think of all this?" Barry asked, an amused curiosity lighting up his brown eyes.

"He thinks it's all our duty to fight the good fight," Gale said nonchalantly. He didn't have the usual energy to feed his patriotic zeal.

"Gotcha," Barry said. Gale looked at Barry and really studied his appearance. He had light olive skin and dark curly hair that was pushed under his uniform helmet. "My dad said the same thing. I think he just wanted to get me out of the house," Barry laughed.

The thought of a father pushing his son to enlist just to get him to move out brought a smile to Gale's face. He had a feeling the two of them would get along just fine. "That could be part of it too, save on tuition," Gale added.

"Yeah, exactly. I think this whole war is just so fathers can get their layabout sons out from underfoot," Barry said, cracking a smile.

Gale rolled the peppermint back and forth in his mouth with his tongue. The longer he sucked on it, the less nauseated he felt. "How'd you know about peppermint stopping nausea?"

Barry shrugged. "Just always have, sorta one of those wives' tales that actually works."

Gale hummed, "You test all of the hangover cures?"

"All but going to bed with wet socks—I can't convince myself it's worth it," Barry said.

"That sounds right. I don't see why it would work," Gale laughed.

"I never said it was a logical one. Just one that existed." Barry leaned over and peered out between the canvas flaps that made up the back of the covered truck. "Any clue where they're taking us?"

"I bet it's the border," Charles piped up, somehow managing to revive himself from the hangover enough to voice his guess.

"That sounds right to me," Gale agreed. "Oh, Barry, this is Charles. Charles, this is Barry." Charles gave a quick wave to Barry, and Barry did the same.

"Make sense. No reason to keep us too far from the front, I suppose. Even though none of us really know what we're doing, 'cept maybe that fellow," Barry said, pointing to Arthur, who had taken the opportunity of sitting in a dark truck to fall asleep.

"Who, Arthur? No, he's a volunteer just like the rest of us," Gale explained.

"Hm, could've fooled me."

"He does that," Charles said. "His stature is deceiving."

The three of them continued to chat as the truck continued to drive forward. The sound of sergeants yelling, engines running, and mechanical grinding and clicking started to fill the air. As the truck slowed down, they could also hear the sound of soldiers marching and drilling. "Must be here," Charles said. He elbowed Arthur. "Hey, wake up!" Gale did the same with Finn that was right next to him. And then he reached over to shove Rory awake. How the three McGuinness brothers managed to sleep on that ride was beyond Gale. Arthur let out a loud yawn and sat up straight, stretching his back. Thomas scooched over beside the former rower, giving him more space to wake up fully. Before anyone could say anything, the canvas flaps were pulled apart, and the sun shined in. Gale blinked his eyes a few times, letting them adjust to the afternoon light after sitting in the dim truck.

"Christ, get a load of that guy," Rory whispered. Rather, attempted to whisper. The whole truck turned to look at him and then the man standing outside of the truck. He was tall and muscular. He had a stony face and dark hair with a streak of gray running through it. He looked disappointed and annoyed as he surveyed the recruits.

"Right," he said, his voice strong and deep. "Welcome to basic, privates. I am your sergeant, Allan Sheppard. You will refer to me as Sergeant or sir at all times? Understand? I will be in charge of your training, and when you pass muster, I will be your commanding officer. Is that understood?"

A couple of the recruits whispered a weak "Yessir." Sheppard seemed like he was beyond unimpressed.

"I said, do you understand?!" he yelled.

"Yes, sir!" every man in the truck yelled back, matching his volume. Gale cringed a bit, the sound making his head hurt all over again.

"Good, now, c'mon. Move out and fall in line," Sheppard said. Slowly, all of the soldiers managed to file out of the truck. Gale reached the edge of the back of the truck and jumped out onto the long grass-covered earth below. He looked around, taking in the camp. They were in the middle of the field, the grass that had been stamped down must be some poor farmer's wheat. Gale felt a bit guilty as he hurried over to line up with the others. He managed to squeeze in between Charles and Rory. He immediately stood at attention. The sergeant started to pace back and forth in the exact same way as the sergeant who had drilled them back in London had. He surveyed them—his blue eyes were piercing and assessing. Gale felt more self-conscious of himself than ever before when the sergeant briefly stopped in front of him. Sergeant Sheppard looked him up and down. "You've had family in the military, private?" he asked.

"Yessir," Gale replied.

"Where did they serve?" he asked, tilting his head to the side. Something told him that depending on his answer, the sergeant was going to judge him worthy or not.

"South Africa and the Crimea, sir," Gale answered.

"Who?"

"My father was in the Boer War, my grandfather in the Crimean War."

The sergeant nodded, seemingly happy with Gale's response and then he continued onward looking down the line. It was then that Gale realized the man was holding a riding crop. He started to wonder if the sergeant was part of the cavalry, and if that was the unit they would be placed in, and then, he realized, Sergeant Sheppard was using it to nudge each recruit into the proper position to stand at attention. He didn't smack or hit the recruit, but he also wasn't afraid to aggressively push them into the right posture. He wasn't going to put up with any nonsense, Gale realized. He was a career sergeant and it showed.

Training on the fly, as it turned out, was not any easier than Gale imagined it. In fact, it seemed that Sergeant Sheppard had decided that because they only had a limited time to train it meant that training days were going to last so long, they would bleed into the next day. In the late hours of the night after the sixth day of training, Gale genuinely thought he'd rather just be in a battle. Surely, war would be less sadistic than the drills Sheppard had designed. But, instead of going to battle, the days of training stretched out in front of them, slowly bleeding into weeks. Every day they were woken by the brassy sound of a bugle horn blaring in the air. At first, Gale thought they woke up around five in the morning. But, after checking his pocket watch, he realized that the hours were different almost every morning. Sometimes it was four, or six. Other days it was even earlier. Sheppard wanted them prepared to fight at any time of the day. "It's not the bloody bank!" he had yelled at his trainees when they were slow one morning to line up. "War doesn't wait for you beauty sleep!"

"We knew that just looking at him," Barry had whispered into Gale's ear. It took everything in his power not to laugh at Barry's comment, but he was unable to stop the amused smirk from crossing his face. However, the sergeant had noticed the exchange before either Gale or Barry could pretend like it didn't happen.

Sheppard had quickly marched over to Gale and Barry, a mask of anger sliding over his face. "What's so funny, boys?" Sheppard asked.

"Nothing, sir," Gale replied, quickly, setting his shoulders back, doing his best to stand at the perfect version of attention.

"I'm sure I can speak for the rest of us," Sheppard started, looking between Barry and Gale, "when I say that we all would like to know. I, for one, love a good laugh. So, please, enlighten us." The sergeant's tone was even more threatening than his words. He leaned into Barry's space. "Well?" he asked.

"Uh, it was nothing, sir," Barry managed to eke out.

"So, you interrupted our training ... for nothing?"

Barry looked around, like he was trying to figure out what the proper response was. Gale looked at him from the corner of his eye as he stood stalk straight, head facing forward. He gave Barry a sympathetic shrug. It was as small and unnoticeable as possible, but Gale hoped that it showed some sort of comradery.

"Yes, sir, sorry, sir," Barry said.

"Keeping tight lipped won't do anything for you," Sheppard said, "tell me now, or training will get worse for everyone."

Sheppard was a fan of group punishment. "In war," Sheppard had started, "the actions of one affect the fate of all." It was one of the first days, Rory and Barry had hit it off immediately and were goofing off. Since then, had made a point of keeping them separated since they had 'Not been able to act like men.'" Gale and the rest of the boys on their team had teased them about it ever since. But now, Gale realized, he might be joining them in the friendly ridicule.

"I said ..." Barry began, hesitant, he didn't want to finish the sentence, Gale couldn't blame him. His hesitation seemed to annoy Sheppard.

"Private Arlington, what did Private Fritz tell you?"

Gale blanched. He swallowed and cleared his throat. "Well, he, uh, was commenting that beauty sleep was not a priority. That was all, sir."

"That's all?" Sheppard looked between them.

Barry and Gale nodded, "Yessir," they said in unison.

The sergeant nodded back. "Right, well, for that complete waste of time, I want fifteen laps around the camp. All of you, go. Now!" He ordered, loudly enough for the entire camp to hear. Gale was certain he heard a captain snicker as he walked by carrying papers. Without another moment of hesitation, the privates began to jog around the camp. There was a path worn in the field, making a perimeter of flattened grass and emerging dirt where the privates had been made to run laps. It must have been a sight to see the newest recruits running at all hours. They had finally received their rifles a few days ago. Until then, they had been using rough wooden replicas, so they'd get used to the feel of a gun in their hands. Apparently, that was an issue for almost all the newest recruits. British arms manufacturers were having problems keeping up with the demand. So, all the newest privates had to make do. Finally, Gale and the rest of his cohort had gotten real ones, the weight of it strapped to his back felt oddly comforting as he ran his laps.

Gale had noticed his body change the more and more training he had gone through. He was more toned and muscular. His shoulders were broader, waist was trimmer. His arms had more defined biceps and forearms. His uniform fit was less tight around him, instead, Gale found himself having to tighten his belt a notch or two. One of the career officers had laughed when he overheard Gale mentioning it during dinner. "That's the British army diet, for you," he had laughed. "Drilling and bad food does a body good," he had continued. Gale had laughed at that point, but then, he couldn't help but wonder what would happen when he was out in the field, in the middle of action, living off of meager rations. His grandfather had mentioned that he ended up having to take a rope to keep his pants on; he had lost so much weight during the war. Would that happen to Gale too? Would he become wiry and sinewy like Finn with corded muscles, created not from natural build, but rather hunger and drive.

As Gale continued to run, he fell into step with his mates, his team. He looked at all of them, jogging to the same beat: Charles, Finn, Rory, Arthur, Barry, and Thomas. The thudding of their footsteps aligned with the beating of his heart, much like his pulse wanted to rocket up, so did he want to quicken his pace. Gale could only hope they would stay together when the training was done. All the others were competent, and he'd trust them, but not in the way he trusted his team. They all had an affinity and camaraderie together that Gale simply didn't have with the other recruits. Gale adjusted the rifle on his shoulder, allowing his chest to expand more with every breath as they continued to run. He no longer got winded as easily with running as he did in the beginning.

Sergeant Sheppard's training drills were exhausting, but they seemed to work. Gale complained about them, just like everyone else, but he'd be the first to admit he was far more battle-ready than he was a few short weeks ago. The end of August had greeted Gale and the rest of his group with rumors of their first taste of war being imminent. The British Expeditionary Forces and the French Army had been pushed back from the borders of France and Belgium after a French retreat. They were now all lingering at the Marne. Something about that position weighed heavily on Gale's mind. He knew that something important was destined to happen there, the same way he was certain that war was only days away from breaking out. Maybe it was because of the stories his grandfather and father had filled his head with as a child. It must have given him an almost sixth sense when it came to war. He wanted nothing more than to be there. He hoped the rumblings of them joining the BEF on the front was some training camp nonsense to keep the recruits entertained.

"It's hardly surprising the French surrendered," Charles said after hearing the news. "If they'd just stood strong like they were meant to, we wouldn't have lost so much territory," Charles continued. He spoke like he was simply musing on the tactics of schoolchildren playing cricket and rugby.

"The Huns must have some impressive sort of army for them to run with their tail between their legs so quickly," Gale agreed. The whole group was sitting outside their tents. A small fire was burning for light and to keep the slight chill of the summer night away. Although, if Gale were honest, he wouldn't mind letting the breeze cool him down. It was hot, and having a break from the sun and the sweat built up from training was refreshing.

"Well, how do you buy a French gun?" Barry started as he was lounging back, smoking a cigarette, resting on his elbow and pack. "Once dropped, never fired." The group laughed, but it was strained, like they all knew the implications of having the French as their closest allies. If the French wouldn't fight, what did that mean for their future?

"Hopefully it's just a fluke at the beginning and the French can find some semblance of a backbone before we all have to step in for them," Gale said, breaking the uncomfortable silence that had fallen after Barry's joke.

"Ah, here's the eternal optimist we all know and put up with," Rory said.

"And what about it?" Gale replied, raising his eyebrow. Ever since they had reached training, Rory's humor had grown just a hair more cynical than ever before. He wasn't sure what had caused it, but Gale wondered what being on the front might do to Rory. Hopefully, it'll make him grow up some.

"Nothing, just thinking that we rely on the frogs, that's all."

"He's got a point," Arthur chimed in, defending his younger brother.

"How so?" Thomas asked. Gale and Charles looked between each other; it was clear they were both thinking the exact same thing. This better not turn into a fight.

Before anyone could say anything else, Sergeant Sheppard walked up to the group. Finn was the first to notice and was quick to start to scramble up to stand at attention. The rest of the group started to follow suit before Sheppard held out his hand. "At ease, gentlemen." The group looked back and forth at each other and slowly let their bodies sink back down into the comfortable position they had been in prior to Sheppard's appearance.

"Right, lads, we've been given our assignments, and you lot are all on my team. Understand?"

"Yessir," they said in quick unison. Gale was relieved his group had made it into one team, even if it meant dealing with Sergeant Sheppard and his exacting, no-nonsense attitude.

"Good, you'll be given a final review by General Foch at dawn to ensure you are ready for the field. Once you pass muster, we'll head out, understand?"

The group looked at each other, a French general was going to be reviewing them? After the conversation they had just had it felt silly to have him sign off on their training. But, instead of saying anything, they all simply said: 'Yessir'.

"Good, head to bed, I refuse to have anyone on my team lagging because they're tired." With that, the sergeant turned on his heel and left without saying another word.

"That was …" Gale started, unsure how to finish the sentence.

"Abrupt," Charles said, completing Gale's thought.

Gale nodded, "Yup."

Thomas stood up, "We should listen to the sergeant, we don't want to look like fools." The rest of the team nodded.

Arthur pulled out his canteen and dumped water over the small flame, effectively extinguishing the fire. The group all stood up and headed to their tents. Gale struggled to fall asleep that night. Nerves and excitement mingled in his blood as it rushed through his veins. His stomach wrestled between feeling like it had a deep pit forming and butterflies churning. He closed his eyes and made himself keep them shut in an attempt to force himself to sleep, but it was to no avail. He tossed and turned, desperate to get comfortable and to get his body to let him pass out. He kept thinking about the story his granddad had told him about the Crimean War. Surely, with their rifles and modern machinery, the war would be far less gruesome. He could hardly imagine what it would be like him to lose his friends the same way his grandad had. That night he swore he would do everything in his power to keep them alive and safe. They were his team, and he would protect their backs, even at the cost of his own. Eventually, he could see the pale gray light start to creep into his tent, indicating that the night was receding as the sun began to climb up from beneath the horizon. He groaned; he really hadn't slept a wink. It was going to be a long day, he knew it. He forced himself to sit up, ignoring the exhaustion that was trying to pull him backward onto the cot. He let himself yawn and stretch, listening to his vertebrae pop one by one. The wood-and-canvas cot was not the most comfortable place to sleep regardless, but, after laying on it for hours, counting down every second, Gale realized it was truly far more unpleasant than he allowed himself to consider it to be in the beginning. He refused to complain about the conditions of the training camp, after all, war wasn't supposed to be comfortable.

Gale finally had enough of his wits about him to get up and get ready. He was certain that in only a few short minutes a loud bugle horn would cut the peace of the camp, alerting the recruits that it was time for the final inspection of their training by the French general. He thought it was a little odd that it wouldn't be a British commander signing off, but war led to strange things, he supposed. He grabbed his pack, making sure that he had carefully wrapped up the family portrait he had brought with him in a cotton uniform shirt. His mother had given it to him, and he was going to make sure to bring it back. Gale stood up, having to duck to make sure he didn't accidentally hit the cloth ceiling of his canvas tent, and staggered outside.

He looked around and realized that it must still be quite early, there was very little movement in the camp. Anxiety briefly gripped him, wondering if he had been left behind, but then the gentle snores of his fellow comrades reassured him. He had never had a chance to look at the camp without a myriad of activities pulling his attention in a million different directions. He took the chance to look around. He took in the stamped-down field of grain that was hosting him, and he wondered for the first time who was the farmer that had sacrificed his land to cause. He hoped whoever it was would be compensated for it. The rows of canvas tents looked peaceful. The large trucks were quiet for once. The silence of the early morning hours was oddly peaceful, he hadn't realized just how used to the loud sounds typical of an army encampment he had gotten. If Gale thought about it, he could hear the phantom sounds of orders being called, of men marching and talking. Or the rumbling engines or trucks or practice fire from guns.

"It's too quiet, isn't it?"

Gale turned around to find the source of the comment—it was Sheppard.

"A bit, sir," Gale replied.

"No need for the sir, not this early. Just call me Sheppard."

"Yes, si—I mean, sure, Sheppard."

"I was never able to sleep the night before we headed out when I was in the BEF," Sheppard began. Gale looked at him and saw the faint tracings of dark circles beginning to form around his eyes. Gale couldn't help but wonder if having an exhausted sergeant was going to cost them. "It's the nerves, they can be the worst impediment on the field if you let it, or if you harness them, you can use them to your advantage. They make your senses sharper, and if you listen to your instincts, you'll know when something is off before the rest of the team. Make sure you use them and not let them get in your way," Sheppard said.

Gale wasn't sure how to respond, so, instead, he just nodded.

"You have potential, you know, all of you do. That's why I'm pushing you lot so hard. It'd be a shame to lose you because you aren't ready for battle." Gale looked at Sheppard and let himself fully survey the man for the first time. He realized the sergeant must have been younger than he acted. He couldn't be older than thirty-five. Much younger than Gale Sr. The lines on his face seemed to be less intense in the morning. His face relaxed as he watched the sun begin to rise. Gale wondered if the sergeant would ever bring this up again. Or, if it was going to be forgotten the moment the sun rose above the horizon and they were to be inspected.

"We got a telegram last night. We're meeting the BEF and the French at the front. Your inspection may just be a baptism under fire." Sheppard looked back at Gale and nodded before he slapped him on the back. "Tell the rest of the team to get up and meet me by that truck," Sheppard said pointing. "We're moving out."

CHAPTER 4

September 3rd-12th, 1914

The march to the Marne was not what Gale expected. First of all, there were far more taxis than he thought there would be. It was a delightful sight to see taxi after Parisian taxi filled with French Army reinforcements. As Gale watched them drive alongside the lines of trucks and men marching to the Marne River valley, he saw the French troops smiling and laughing, and he realized that most of them had probably never been in a taxi. Gale had only been in an automobile taxi a handful of times and that was when Charles had been too drunk to drive them back from whatever pub they had found themselves in at the end of the night.

"What a sight that is, eh? Bet the Germans never thought the taxis would come to the rescue," Rory laughed, leaning over the wooden slats that made up the side of their truck. He waved at a couple of the French soldiers in the taxi next to them. The soldiers waved right back. The sun was shining down, and the day was becoming warm and bright. It felt surreal as Gale leaned against the side of the truck. It trundled along the dirt road, kicking up dirt, making a golden-brown haze in the air that seemed to suspend around the green wheat fields. In that moment, it made sense to Gale why so many great artists hailed from France. The rolling hills and lush fields were hypnotizingly beautiful; it made Gale wish he knew how to draw or paint. He wanted to capture the beauty before the inevitable destruction. He hoped there was someone somewhere in the countless numbers of troops all heading toward Marne who was committing the surreal scene of taxis carrying troops with trucks pulling machine guns behind them over the French countryside to memory to draw at night. It was strange, they were barely thirty miles out from Paris, and it felt like they were worlds away. The relative peacefulness of the drive was short-lived as the smell of smoke and gunpowder started to fill Gale's nose, it burned, and he wanted to sneeze.

Had the battle already broken out?

Gale leaned out and saw all the jocular laughter and shouting of all the other troops had suddenly ceased. He looked forward and saw troops quickly lining up. Smoke was floating toward them, carried westward by the wind. Proof of the battles and the German advance. It was then that Gale realized their destination was not the Marne as he had already anticipated. It was, rather, further southwest. The Germans had made it much further than Gale had realized. He turned to look at the rest of his team, and he realized they had the same shocked response. No longer were they leaning back, letting the wind ruffle through their hair. Nor were they laughing. It was just like the rest of the troops out of the truck. Gale turned to the sergeant. He was inhaling deeply, his mouth was set into a straight line. He rolled his shoulders back, and Gale realized that this was the battle-hardened version of the Sheppard that he had seen hints of. He didn't seem artificially intense as he had while he was training them.

The convoy slowed to a stop and Sergeant Sheppard stood and walked to the end of the truck and turned to look at his team. "Alright, men, this is as far as the truck is going, time to move out." Without another word, the sergeant easily hopped out the end of the truck and continued to move forward without missing a single step. One by one, the team filed out of the truck. When Gale's boots hit the ground, he was immediately struck by the sheer amount of men he saw. The earth was cut up and trampled, dirt and mud exposed by the hundreds and thousands of footprints and wheel marks. He was thankful for the gaiters that covered his boots and kept the dirt from clinging to his pants. The sun was still shining just as brightly as it was earlier, and for some reason that was unclear to Gale, that felt strange. He was walking into battle, the nerves and excitement from the night before had returned, giving him a strange, giddy feeling. He rolled his shoulders back and tried to focus on the advice that Sheppard had given him that morning. *Don't let your nerves take over, use them to stay sharp.* He adjusted the rifle that was slung over his shoulder, his fingers worrying over the leather strap and metal buckle. The team got into line. Gale standing shoulder to shoulder with Charles. His brother in all but blood. The two looked at each other. This was it, they were going to prove themselves.

The rest of the day faded into a blur; Gale went through the motions of the proper soldiers, doing as he was ordered and falling into line. Eventually, Sergeant Sheppard received their orders and they headed out to the front. Before the battle began, there was silence, or maybe Gale simply imagined the silence, and then there was the sound of a loud pop and whiz. A scream. The battle had begun. Gale and the others loaded their rifles, aimed, and fired. Dirt was being kicked up by stray bullets. Then there was a loud crashing sound, followed by an explosion. A large artillery shell shot out from behind the German lines. It arched through the air, smoke trailing behind it. The shell exploded as it buried itself into the ground. Shrapnel and other debris shot out in every direction. Gale's ears were ringing from the noise, and he silently thanked God that his team was just out of the way. But, as Gale looked across the field and through the smoke, Gale realized that a line of artillery was forming just behind the German front. He turned to see the sergeant hunkered down in place with the rest of the team. He was reloading his rifle, his hands moving deftly with a familiarity that only comes from years of practice and use. The rest of the team was slow and fumbling. Gale turned his attention back to the battle and loaded his own rifle. His hands shook as he grabbed his stripper clip, pulled the bolt back, and inserted rounds. He took a deep breath and lifted his rifle and placed it tightly against his shoulder. As he exhaled, he pulled the trigger. The kickback didn't surprise him like it did the first time he had shot it in training. He watched the bullet fly into the smoke-filled fray.

All the sounds on the battlefield seemed to mute, the screaming of pain, the yelling of orders, the mechanical sound of engines and gears, the clicking of guns, and explosives detonating. Gale's gaze tracked the movement of the bullet as it struck the shoulder of a German shoulder.

"Nice shot, mate!" Charles yelled from the left of Gale.

Gale turned and watched as Charles shot his own rifle, hitting another soldier from across the field. "You too!" Gale yelled back.

The two continued to shoot side by side. Out of the corner of his eye, Gale kept checking in with what was going on with the McGuinnesses, Barry, and Thomas. Another member of their team was added last minute, an eighteen-year-old named Michael Aleman. He was serious and contemplative. When Gale met him at training, he wanted to ask him why the hell he volunteered. He reminded Gale of Finn, and Finn would not have enlisted without being cajoled. It worried Gale that he was alone without any friends, but luckily, he was certain that Michael would fit in with the rest of the Sheppard team. They were all in line as they were trained shooting and reloading as quickly as they could. It was impressive how in sync they all were, naturally. While half of them were shooting, the other half were reloading. They were constantly on the defense, doing their best to push forward against the Germans.

Another artillery shell exploded, but this time it was much closer. The earth shook with its impact, and Gale could feel the heat of the explosive wave. His ears were ringing painfully, but Gale continued on shooting, doing his best to keep shooting despite the disorientation. Before he could get another shot out, he heard a whizzing noise, and hot pain erupted from the side of his face. Gale reached out and felt the spot just above his ear. It was covered in blood, and he prodded it gingerly. It wasn't a deep wound. Then, Gale realized that he had been grazed by a bullet. His heart started thudding in his chest.

"Arlington!" Sheppard yelled, drawing Gale's attention to . "You alright?"

Gale nodded, unsure how else to respond. He wasn't going to die from the injury; it was barely worse than a badly scraped knee. But head wounds bleed a lot, and he could feel blood dripping down the side of his face. He was careful to hold his head in a way that he wouldn't get any of it into his right eye. Before he realized what was happening, Sheppard was by his side. The sergeant grabbed Gale's face and tilted it slightly to the side so the sun could illuminate the injury better. Gale blinked the blood from his eye as it dripped across his face. The sergeant pulled out a roll of bandages. "Field medics are a bit busy with worse wounds," Sheppard said, he had to yell to be heard over the sound of battle and the ringing in Gale's ears. It was then that Gale realized Sheppard had been even closer to the artillery shell than he was. But before Gale could check to see if the sergeant was fine, the older man wrapped his injury. He then turned to the rest of the team that was already looking over. "Don't get distracted! We got to hold the line!"

"Yessir!" they all yelled.

Gale lifted his rifle back up, he slid over closer to the rest of the lads. He was surprised when Sheppard stepped closer too. The team formed a tight unit. Between the nine of them, the group was making progress shooting down and rebuffing any German defense. Hours passed, and Gale was exhausted. He had no idea how much longer they were going to be fighting but, however long it took, Gale was willing to keep fighting. He reached into his pouch holding his rounds and realized he was low on bullets.

"Dammit," Gale yelled. "I'm almost out!"

"Here!" Charles reached into his ammo pouch and shoved a large handful of bullets into Gale's.

"How do you have any left?!" Gale asked as he loaded the magazine.

"I'm just that good!" Charles replied.

"Hey, less yelling, more shooting boys!" Sheppard ordered, his voice bellowing over the sound of guns firing.

Gale and Charles immediately turned back to the front and continued to fire. Gale steeled his nerves as he watched the cannons on the German side be reloaded. He braced himself as another barrage of artillery shells were shot toward the British lines. All around him were men screaming as they were hit with shrapnel. It was surreal to think that every bang he heard could possibly result in the death or injury of his fellow soldier. Gale refused to even think about the implications of his own firing. He had to think about it as a way to stop the German advance, nothing more nothing less. They had to stop the Huns from taking over France.

Eventually Gale noticed that between the firing of the cannons, as he peered through the flying debris and thick smoke, there were fewer and fewer individual soldiers firing pistols and rifles at them. They weren't making an attempt to advance anymore. In fact, the only German soldiers that Gale could see were the ones manning the cannons. Something wasn't right, and it was setting Gale on edge.

"Sarge!" Gale yelled, shuffling over to Sheppard.

"Yes, Private Arlington?" It was almost funny how formal their conversation already sounded while they were literally trying to avoid being blown up.

"All the soldiers are gone, sir!"

"What?"

"Look, it's just the artillery!" Gale said, nodding in the direction of the cannons.

Sheppard looked over across the line, realization dawning on his face. "They're trying to flank us and the French. We need to move! Men, time to move out, let's go!" Sheppard waved the team over and began to march off.

The battle kept going. And going. It felt endless, each time they made progress, the Germans began to fight back. It was like their numbers were endless. But, the British and French were holding their own. General Foch had picked up on the same movement that Gale had. The Germans were trying to maneuver themselves through a gap in between the French and British defenses. General Foch formed the ninth army almost a fortnight ago, and they were finally joining up with them. Finally, they had pushed the Germans back to the River Marne. Gale was certain they were going to succeed, but they couldn't let up.

Exhaustion dragged at Gale, his movements were sluggish. Even though Sheppard's team had been able to catch a bit of a shut-eye, it didn't really seem to be making much difference. Gale wasn't sure what day it was, it was at least the tenth, or maybe it was already the twelfth. The day started out as it usually did. They ate their rations quickly, the tough dried meat and bread made Gale miss the days of the training camp mess. Who knew that was possible? It didn't take long for them to get back into the fray. Every day played out similarly to the first day of the battle. But now, instead of the Germans trying to outflank them, they were facing the BEF and French army full on. The amount of cannons and bullets sent their way was astronomical. But Gale and the rest of the army met each shot blow for blow. They were not going to lose land. Germany was not going to be able to seize any more territory.

The team was lined up shooting. Everyone was confident, only a little worse for wear. It was time for the final push. They had their orders, having crossed the Marne with the rest of the British and French forces pushing the Germans further and further back toward Belgium and Germany. Gale had his rifle pressed against his shoulder, the wood was warm from picking up his body heat. The weight of it was familiar and comforting now. He dreaded the day that he had to use the bayonet and his army knife. But, for now, he was fine with locking and loading his gun. He used the sight as a way for him to confirm where he was already aiming. Over the past few days his aim had gotten especially good. Sheppard had even pointed it out, in his own way.

He thought the day was going to be another normal one. They were all hunkered down behind an overturned truck that had been hit with cannon fire. It seemed like a safe position. It was a safe position. Everyone aside from Arthur and Charles had to stretch to see over the bed of the truck. He was about to pull the trigger when he heard a sickening ripping and squelching noise. It took Gale a second to realize what that sound was. He turned and saw Michael stumble backward and fall to the ground. He was about to ask if he was okay, to reach into his pocket and pull out some extra bandages to offer him. Gale thought he must have just been grazed by the bullet. But, as he looked at Michael laying on the ground, his pale skin staining red as blood spilled from a ragged hole in the middle of his forehead. The rest of the team had turned around and had looked to see what had happened right along with Gale.

"Steady! Stay in place, keep firing!" Sheppard yelled. When no one did as he said he continued. "That's an order, privates! Keep firing, we can't let up, not now!"

Gale felt a chill run down his spine as he and the rest of the team mechanically turned around and started to shoot again. Their motions were automatic at this point. Gale was grateful they had magazines and the rifles could take five rounds before having to be reloaded. He felt like everything was numb. He knew he didn't have a choice but to keep fighting. When Gale had signed up for war, he did so with his eyes open. Or what he had thought to be open. He had dealt with death before. He'd been to funerals. Looked at his own grandmother's cold body during the wake. She had looked small and overly pale, almost gray. There was no evidence in her that she had once breathed, had blood pumping through her body. Or even that she was animate. At that point, he supposed, she had been embalmed. Despite the rouge they had put on her face, it looked like it was a mannequin or a wax figure at Madame Tussauds. This was different. One moment, Michael was only a few feet away, stretching up on his tiptoes to get a good angle to shoot at Germans, and the next he was on the ground. Gale wanted to turn and check on him, check his pulse, try to breathe life back into him or stop the blood that was still leaking out from the bullet hole. But it would be pointless. He already knew Michael was dead. There was no way he would survive that. Even if Gale did turn and check, he knew that the sergeant would only yell at him or find some sort of punitive punishment to get back at him for disobeying direct orders.

However, out of the corner of Gale's eye, he saw the sergeant turn down and check on Michael. He checked his pulse and hovered his hand over his mouth, checking for any breath or sign of life. Anything that he could use to justify calling the medic over to check on the private. Michael was the youngest of the team. He was a violinist, studying at the Royal College of Music. He must have been talented. He had promised to play something for them if they had ever came across a violin that he could play in their time on the front. Gale thought that it would be possible. There were plenty of French towns, and they would probably be near Paris soon after the battle to get some rest before the next.

Now Gale realized that would not be happening. He would never get to hear Michael play the fiddle reel that he always hummed under his breath while he was checking his supplies. Gale continued to fire at the Germans, a new fury boiling in his stomach. How dare they take the life of someone that had so much promise? He continued to watch Sheppard's movements. The man gently closed Michael's empty gray eyes and crossed him. Then, after a beat the sergeant grabbed Michael's dog tags and then reached into the interior pocket of the private's jacket and pulled out a couple folded envelopes. Gale knew what the contents of the envelopes were. They were a mix of letters intended for their loved ones and ones they had received from them. All of them had them in their breast pocket. It was standard, they were told to write one at the beginning of basic. None of them had actually thought those letters would need to be sent. But now, watching Sheppard deftly place the letters in his front pocket for safe-keeping, Gale realized just how real it was. But it wasn't the time to be a scared little boy. He wasn't a child. He was nineteen, almost twenty. He was here to become a man and he had to fight through the nausea of his realization and keep going. It was time for him to employ the proverbial British stiff upper lip and fight on for Michael.

The day dragged on and finally, *finally*, the Germans seemed to be retreating. They followed them, forcing them to keep moving, to keep pushing them back. They were going to retake all they could until they were eventually ordered to stop. All the troops were exhausted. Supplies were depleted as they pushed the German line back, they were moved further and further away from the supply lines based in Paris.

That night the team sat around a fire. Sheppard was off, somewhere. Gale assumed relaying the news of Michael's death and passing on his letters. The chill that had run down Gale's back earlier returned. Gale shook his head and rolled his shoulders to get rid of it.

"You good there, mate?"

Gale looked up and saw Thomas's concerned gaze fixed on him from across the fire. Gale realized that he had no right to be as affected by Michael's death. After all, Thomas had gotten closer. They were standing next to each other. After the final push, it was Thomas that had to wash off Michael's blood and brain matter that had splattered on him.

"I'm doing just fine, thanks," Gale replied, offering Thomas a tight smile.

"Right, well, I'm doing bloody awful," Rory said as he tuned into their conversation, "and I think you're a liar, Gale."

"I'm doing just fine," Gale pushed back.

"Sure you are. You usually look like your two shades away from being as green as grass," Charles chimed in.

"You do look a bit rough," Finn added quietly.

"I think I'm doing just as well as you lot. It wasn't easy, 'specially not today," Gale finally conceded. He knew it was easier than to argue with his friends. They were just as stubborn as he was, and they were in the majority. He had zero chance of winning the small argument that was brewing. Besides, he didn't really have the energy for it.

"Think they've found him yet?" Thomas asked after a beat.

"Surely, they must've," Arthur said, nodding his head a bit like he was convincing himself.

"There's a lot to be found ..." Charles said, trailing off a bit.

"Sheppard got his letter," Gale said, "and his dog tags, that's what really matters, right?" Gale tried not to think about the long trek back of all the deceased soldiers. He didn't envy those assigned to collecting the bodies and sending them back. He wondered if there were even people doing that.

"Yeah, you're right," Barry said. "Look, I know it's a somber night, but look at how far back we pushed the Huns. This war is sure to be over by Christmas, just like they promised."

"Definitely," Gale agreed, "and until then, we'll all have each other's backs."

The rest of the team agreed.

"That we will." Gale turned around to see Sheppard standing behind them. He had a look to his face that was somehow more solemn and more serious than any other look that Gale had ever seen on him.

"We've been given instructions to start digging trenches, lads. Us and the rest of the troops around here. We'll dig them to these specifications". He held out a hastily drawn looking schematic, "And as we build ours, we'll link it to those beside us. Seems like we're going to be here for the long haul. So get some rest, we start to dig tomorrow, got it?"

"Yessir," the team says in unison. They were getting good at that, Gale thought. But, after a couple months of responding to Sergeant Sheppard's proclamation it was automatic.

The next few weeks passed on quickly. They dug and dug and dug until they had managed to build a trench that was eight feet deep and six feet wide. At some point a group of soldiers had come by with a significant amount of sandbags to place on the parapet. "They'll help absorb some of the gunfire," Finn had surmised. He had then suggested they take wooden slats from destroyed vehicles and crates to line their sleeping dugouts.

"We need to keep as much water out as we can, right?" he added quietly.

Sheppard thought that was a fantastic idea and ran with it. He grabbed Arthur and they came back with enough wooden slats to line the entire trench they had dug. It was so well done that other teams began to notice. Some tried to follow suit, but it quickly became clear that they had limited supplies of wood and other insulating materials.

"You are a bloody genius for figuring that out," Barry had said, slapping Finn on the back.

"Seriously, you are the brains of this outfit," Gale agreed. Even though most of their attention was fixed on building up their trench and making it as fortified as they possibly could, the warfare didn't cease. They were, after all, only a few hundred meters away from the German army. It was inevitable that as both sides built their defenses they would trade shots back and forth. Each of them had received assignments from Sheppard in addition to helping with the trenches. Charles, Finn, and Barry were made to be sappers, they were to focus their energy full time on digging the trenches. It seemed like exhausting work. Gale couldn't help but laugh as Charles' clean-cut, posh boy persona was quickly chipped away at the longer he spent in the dirt digging. In addition to digging, they were also instructed to help with laying barbed wire—a job that Charles jumped at.

"Anything to get out of that bloody trench. If I have to spend one more evening picking dirt from under my fingernails, I'll swear I'll—" he never finished his proclamation as Sheppard pushed them on into No Man's land. It was dangerous. German's were aiming at them all the time. Charles was the best shot, so he kept watch as Finn and Barry deftly cut and laid out the wires, traps, and mines. He would shoot any German that so much as looked in their direction. Charles was as good as a shot as Gale was. Now it seemed like they were going to be in friendly competition to see who really was the best shot until the war ended. The team all took bets, and they all seemed to be split on it.

Rory and Arthur were assigned to man the machine gun that was perched upon the parapet. It was movable but heavy. Arthur was really the only one that could navigate moving it with ease, that's why he was in charge of it. Rory was meant to feed the magazines while Arthur shot. The machine guns were a great boon in keeping any German soldier back from setting their own mines and traps. Although, they had their own that were trying to pick off people like

Charles, Finn, and Barry. They were literally putting their lives on the line every time they went out. Gale and Thomas were assigned support to the machine gun. Keep an eye on soldiers trying to take the gun out or those manning it. It wasn't said, but both Gale and Thomas knew it was their job to take over in case Arthur and Rory were incapacitated in anyway temporarily ... or permanently.

One night, things were quiet. The team was sitting around another fire, eating soup that they had managed to make out of their rations. Apparently, a mess was being built somewhere in the trench, but Gale wasn't sure how true that rumor was. He'd believe it when he saw it. Until then, he was grateful to have the beef somewhat reconstituted. He was genuinely worried that he was going to break his teeth on the rations.

The group was sitting in silence. It was another hard day, and they were all exhausted. They had just about completed their trench that day, just a little more digging until they met the others. It seemed like they had been digging their trenches out for ages at this point. Sheppard cleared his throat, drawing attention from the team.

"We've been told to name our positions, to help keep things straight at HQ," he started. "I have a suggestion of a name, but we should all agree." Sheppard, as it turned out, was far more democratic on the battlefield than his attitude in training had suggested. He paused for a moment, then said, "Fiddler's Crossing."

Each man in the group knew exactly why he chose that name. It was in honor of Michael. Their first, and hopefully, only casualty on the team.

"I like it," Gale said, "it's ... distinctive."

"I agree," Charles said. "For Michael."

"For Michael," the rest of the team murmured, like they were hesitant to say it any louder.

"I'll report it back to our superiors, then. Glad we're all in agreement," Sheppard said, his voice had taken on a slightly softer tone than Gale had ever thought that it could. His face held the ever stoic and stony expression that Gale had gotten used to seeing. But, in the orange firelight, he could just catch a gentle glint to Sheppard's gaze that made Gale realize that he too was just as affected by the loss of Michael. It made sense, after all, as he was the one to train the violinist. Gale hoped that somewhere, looking down at them, Michael realized that he would be remembered and carried with them to the bitter end. Gale simply hoped that none of them would meet the same fate as Michael as they hunkered down for the night in their newly dubbed Fiddler's Crossing.

CHAPTER 5

October 16th-18th, 1914

One day, as the team was hunkering in for the evening, preparing their rations for the night, Sheppard received a message from a tired-looking private. It was clear that he had been running back and forth and playing messenger all day. Something big was going on. Were they going to be moving? Was there going to be another big battle? Gale wasn't sure what it was, but from the way Sheppard's eyebrows shot up, he knew that it was going to involve all of them. The sergeant looked at the soldier while folding up the missive.

"Thank you, Private Madison, is that all?" Sergeant Sheppard asked.

"Yes, sir," Private Madison said.

"Very good, dismissed." The private took off half walking half jogging just as Sheppard managed to finish the word dismissed.

"Arlington, Dunford, Abbey, with me!" the sergeant ordered.

Barry and the McGuinnesses gave Gale, Charles, and Thomas a questioning look. Gale gave them a shrug in return. He was, after all, just as confused as they were. His mind raced as he tried to figure out what Sheppard would want with them and just what was in the missive that made him call them over. The sergeant walked down through the trench until they reached the dugout they all slept in. Sheppard nodded for them to join him there. He wanted to make sure they wouldn't be overheard by the others.

Gale couldn't help but wonder why they were being pulled aside. Did they do something wrong? Were they going to get a formal reprimand? Were they not doing the duties as soldiers to the satisfactions of the higher-ups? Or were they going to be enlisted into the intelligence-gathering arm of the war. Gale's mind raced with images from the spy novels he had read while at school, Conrad's *The Secret Agent* and Childers' *The Riddle of Sands*. Gale had always thought that he would be a good spy, he had the sort of poker face that was needed, and he had it on good authority he could be quite charming when he wanted to be. Although, he wouldn't be an Agent Provocateur type, no, he'd be more moral than that. He'd do what was right, live by the honorable soldier's code that he was brought up with.

His daydreams were cut short as Sheppard cleared his throat.

Over the months, Gale had come to recognize that was the sergeant's easy way of getting their attention without yelling. It had reached the point that Gale would turn his head to pay attention to the sergeant when he was simply clearing his throat to stop a cough or after he had taken a drag from a particularly rough cigarette. *Pavlov and his dogs would be proud*, Gale thought.

"We have received orders to rendezvous with troops up north in Belgium," Sheppard began, "in Ypres," he added.

Gale had been hearing murmurings from others in the trenches about Ypres. The race to the sea. It was going to be one of those battles that defined how the war went, of that, Gale was certain. Ypres was near some of the key supply ports on the English Channel. Not to mention they needed to take that town or the Germans might be able to outflank them. Or, at least, that was Gale's thought. The longer Gale was in the army, the more he realized that the higher-ups didn't really explain their reasonings or strategies to anyone with a rank lower than Major. At first, he had assumed that at least Sergeant Sheppard got their reasoning, but one night he had said the contrary when Gale had asked why they didn't keep pursuing the Germans.

"We were right on their tail, we could've chased the Huns back before they could say *gesundheit*," Gale had said. Perhaps he was pushing too much with a superior officer, but he felt like he had to ask. It seemed ridiculous for them to get stuck in for so long near the Marne.

"Your guess is as good as mine, Private. Just because I command this team, doesn't mean I'm privy to the strategy behind them."

Now, looking at Sheppard, it seemed obvious that he only received orders and not their reasoning. Any explanation the sergeant offered them was pure speculation grounded in a few more years in the army than they had. "I pulled you three aside because I know you'll be able to stand your ground. You've proven yourself over the last few weeks, and I believe that you three would be the best."

"We're not all going?" Gale asked, unable to stop himself.

"We're not all going, sir," Sheppard corrected. Before Gale could apologize, he continued, "No, private, the whole team will not be coming along. I was surprised too, but they need to make sure that things are covered here too. Besides, they only need reinforcements to bulk up the boys up north. Not an entire army," Sheppard explained. It was obvious from Sheppard's tone that he was just as unhappy as the rest of them were with it. Gale stole a quick glance over at Charles and Thomas, meeting their gaze. It was going to feel weird heading out without Arthur, Finn, Rory, and Barry. Gale was even more surprised that the sergeant hadn't elected Arthur to come along instead of him or Charles. Surely it would have made more sense for the older and calmer members of the team to go along.

"Is that a complaint, Private Arlington?"

Gale blanched, he hadn't realized he had said any of that out loud. Perhaps exhaustion was getting to him more than he had realized. His father had warned before he left that he would never feel as tired and as foggy-headed as during the down days of a battle. It was becoming hard for Gale to sleep when there wasn't the occasional sound of gunfire or the echoes of a skirmish. It made him feel uneasy, like something was off. He wondered if his father or grandad still struggled with it. If they did, they never said anything to Gale, that was certain.

"No, sir, not at all, sir. Just trying to understand."

"Your role is to follow orders, not understand them. Understand?"

Gale saw Charles's lip twitch, suppressing laughter at the contradiction from the sergeant's statement. "Yessir," Gale said, knowing that if he did put a toe out of line, he would be off the mission and that would be devastating. The sergeant trusted him to be competent enough to carry his own weight and fight at a battle that was certain to be strategically important to how the rest of the war played out. If they were able to secure the ports and outflank the Germans, the war would soon be over, surely. Just as the enlistment officers had promised. A small fire of hope was kindled in his stomach as he thought about it. The idea of fighting in a battle that would seal the fate of his fellow countrymen alongside his best friend excited Gale. This time they would be able to prove their worth as soldiers and really fight, not just hide behind a trench wall, shooting rounds across No Man's land in a vain effort to hit a German soldier.

"Right, well, if you all understand, you are dismissed," Sheppard said, seemingly satisfied with Gale's response and the others' quiet nods. The three began to file out when Sheppard called out. "Private Arlington, send along Private McGuinness," he said, then before Gale could ask which one he added, "Arthur McGuinness."

"Right away, sir," Gale replied. With a wave from the sergeant pressing him on, Gale turned on his heel and headed back to the group, quickly catching up with Charles and Thomas.

"We're actually going to fight, lads," Gale said.

"We've been fighting this whole time, Gale," Charles replied, emphasizing Gale's name in a way that made it clear what he meant was idiot.

"You know what I mean, Dunford. Real combat. We're leaving the trenches and we're going to see a proper battle."

"I don't know what you're so excited about," Thomas said. "We've been fighting on the front line this whole time. I doubt we'll all be making it back from Ypres," he added. There was a distinctive gloominess in Thomas's voice.

"But, we signed up for this. This is our chance to really prove ourselves, the sarge wouldn't choose us if he didn't think we were worthy, right?"

"Right," Charles agreed, nodding his head.

Gale and Charles looked at Thomas expectantly.

"Right," Thomas said reluctantly. His tone was still unhappy sounding. Gale wondered if that had to do with Michael. Thomas had taken him under his wing like a little brother in the days they were fighting at the Marne. Gale knew it was difficult for him, even though he'd never say it.

"We'll stand and fight together, the honorable way. Not from behind a wall. But face to face. Proper soldiers. We'll have each other's backs, I swear," Gale said, doing his best to encourage Thomas. Gale clapped Charles and Thomas on the backs as they neared the rest of the team. "Arthur, Sarge wants a word!" he called out, having to speak over an exchange of gunfire. It amazed Gale how used to the sounds of shooting they had all become. It barely phased them at this point.

"Got it," Arthur replied, getting up. "Any idea what about?"

"Dunno," Gale said, "he told us that we're heading to Ypres tomorrow. Going to join up with the detachment up there. Hold the flank or something," he continued.

Arthur looked at them, brow furrowed, like he was trying to figure out what the sergeant could possibly want with him now that those orders had been issued. "Good to know, he say what time?"

"No clue," Charles said, "but knowing the sergeant, I'm betting on dawn." The rest of the team laughed at that. Dawn was Sheppard's favorite time for them to do anything. Everything was at dawn, when the sun was barely shining, and couldn't play witness to the obscene list of orders they had to get through by the end of the day.

Arthur chuckled and headed toward Sheppard's dugout. The group sat around, waiting for his return. After all, what were they supposed to be doing? They didn't have any orders left to do. The sergeant was in the middle of giving them their next tasks when the private had shown up. Gale hoped that it was an order to get a good night's sleep. But somehow, he knew he wouldn't be able to rest until they made it to Ypres. It was going to be just like the night before they shipped out to the Marne. He was going to be on edge, filled with excitement and nerves over what he would be met with when he arrived. He tried to imagine what Belgium would look like, after all, he had never been. Maybe it would look like France? After all, the countries did border each other. How much different could they be? It wasn't like Belgium was a huge territory, so there couldn't be that much room for the country to look vastly different, surely.

Charles was in the middle of telling a bawdy story about a girl he had been seeing on the sly. Her name was Alice, and Gale had heard the tale a few times now. Charles had a tendency to break it out and tell it when he was bored. But, the way he editorialized the tale each time made it interesting to listen to. It wasn't necessarily that he changed the facts, he just made moments more dramatic, more over-the-top, funnier, even, than they were. It was the kind of story that would make you snort out your beer if you were unfortunate enough to be taking a drink as he reached the punchline about the hayloft breaking. For the record, the hayloft didn't break, one of the beams cracked. Gale knew this because Charles had dragged him out of bed that fateful night to help repair it before Alice's father could wake up and see the damage. That was the part that Charles tended to leave out, but Gale didn't mind, he'd always tack it on at the end, ensuring the rapt listeners got the entire picture.

Charles was just getting to the part about climbing up to the hayloft when Arthur and Sheppard returned.

The sergeant cleared his throat, as usual, gaining the attention of the team. "As I'm sure you've heard, I'm taking a few members of our unit with me to act as reinforcements at Ypres. While I'm gone, Private McGuinness will be in charge. I will inform HQ when I leave that is so and he will be given the missives. I expect you listen to his orders as you do mine. Understood?"

"Yessir," they all said in unison.

"Good," Sheppard said. "Arlignton, Dunford, Abbey, pack up. We leave in an hour."

That was a surprise. Usually, they had more time. It was in the evening. Perhaps they were to be taking a train. Gale hoped so. At least then he would be able to get some sleep. The idea of marching all the way to Belgium or taking a truck sounded distinctly unpleasant. Sheppard left, presumably to back his own kit up and fill the pouches of the vest they called webbing. The webbing was handy, Gale did have to admit, even though it was heavy. Not having to tote around a bag during battle and keep track of the small portrait he had in his back pocket set him at ease. There was something about always having it within reach that made Gale grateful he took it with him. Carrying his family by his side while he was fighting with his brothers in arms made sense to him.

"I can't believe I have to listen to Artie," Rory complained. "The whole point of coming to war was to get out of your bloody shadow."

"Maybe grow a few more inches and you'll have a chance," Arthur replied.

"Hey! I'm not short!"

"You're just like a terrier," Arthur laughed. "Small, loud, and brazen."

"Sod off," Rory replied.

"Oh, I can completely see that," Barry said, between laughs. "I for one am looking forward to your command, Acting Sergeant Artie."

While the others laughed, Gale, Charles and Thomas set about making sure they had what they needed for the coming days. They packed their rations, ammunition, personal effects, rifle pull through, field dressing, cards, and cigarettes. *The necessities*, Gale thought as he made sure to check his box of matches to ensure he had enough for the coming days. He did not want to get stuck in Belgium without a way to light a cigarette. He had become a much more avid smoker as the days had worn on. It soothed his nerves at the end of a long day and quelled any hunger he might have been having. Besides, what else was there to do? There were only so many rounds of gin rummy he could play before he got bored.

When it came time for them to head out, they said their goodbyes to the rest of the team.

"We'll see you again soon, just have to deal with Jerry first," Gale said, waving at the others.

"Give a what for for me!" Rory yelled as they left, making Gale, Charles, Thomas, and even Sheppard laugh.

The evening sun was just starting to set as they headed toward the idling truck. Gale's hopes of a train transport were quickly dashed. *However, at least this truck was covered,* Gale thought. They wouldn't be as exposed to the elements as he had been before. At this point, it was a small mercy, but a mercy nonetheless. Gale filled on after the sergeant. Charles followed him, and Thomas brought up the rear. Gale placed his rifle on top of his knees and leaned back against the metal poles that held the canvas cover in place. He let his eyes slide close as the truck began to drive off.

Gale and the rest managed to get a bit of shut-eye before they arrived just a few miles west of the Ypres. It was immediately obvious when they arrived. Before Gale even opened his eyes, he could hear the sound of troops drilling and machine gears grinding, all mixed with the familiar smell of gunpowder and soldiers in need of a bath—it couldn't be anything else but the camp. Gale groaned and opened his eyes. He looked around and had a strange feeling of déjà vu as he looked around the truck. It was a similar scene from when he first arrived at the Marne. He looked to Thomas and Charles, and it was clear that they were feeling the same as him. None of them knew what to expect when they went outside. It sounded the same as the trenches. He knew that there were trenches in Ypres. It seemed that the entire western front was going to be fought from the trenches at this point.

Sheppard stood up the second the truck lurched to a stop. "Let's move out. Orders from command will be waiting for us at the command tent." Without another word, Sheppard stepped out of the truck with a practiced ease. Gale, along with Charles and Thomas, quickly followed. When they set foot on the ground, Gale was immediately struck by just how dark it was. There were no lights, not even from campfires.

"I'm going to fall in the bloody trench and break my ankle," Gale muttered to Charles.

"Not the most heroic way to get injured," he replied, mirth in his tone.

"No, by my estimation it's just a bit better than being shot in the foot, I would say," Gale laughed. He didn't feel bad about being loud, even though it was late and dark, the yelling voices of sergeants drilling their team and the rest of the cacophonous sounds that came from an army gearing up for battle did little to preserve the peaceful sanctity of night. He was certain that the Germans were gearing up in just the same way. Gale couldn't help but wonder how many cannons and machine guns they had on both sides. It was worrying to consider. He only had about seventy bullets, and had a feeling that if he did end up needing more, he would have to scavenge through the injured and deceased for them. He had seen other soldiers doing that in the midst of battle, and Sheppard didn't seem to think it was out of the ordinary.

They zig-zagged around the trenches, walking over wooden planks that were placed over the trenches as a makeshift bridge. The slat of wood Gale was walking over creaked a bit with every step. From behind him, Thomas cursed. "I'm just waiting for this damn thing to break under us."

"Have a problem, Private Abbey?" Sheppard asked from just up ahead.

"No sir," Thomas replied, nerves obvious in his voice. Thomas was rarely called out by the sergeant, he was usually doing exactly what he needed to be doing without any complaint, so he didn't draw much attention to himself, and Gale was pretty sure that was how he liked it too. Charles and Gale snickered at the interaction, it was nice to see the teacher's pet get chastised for once.

"Right, command should be just right around here," Sheppard said as he took a sharp left. Suddenly, as Gale and the others followed their sergeant, a canvas tent came into view. It was gently illuminated from the inside out by small gas lamps inside, or possibly just candles. Gale wasn't sure. Who knew what the commanders had available to them. As they neared the tent, Sheppard turned around and faced them. "Wait here," he said, then as an afterthought, "I mean it." Then he went into the tent.

"Where would we even go?" Charles asked, annoyance clear in his voice. "We can't make out Adam from Eve out here."

"Sometimes I think if he could tie us to a post like a posh lady's dog, I think he would," Thomas laughed.

"I could see him doing that," Gale agreed, "although, it's not like we've done anything to deserve it."

"I think he has nightmares of us running off. I guess he's decided not to take a chance on reality," Charles shrugged. He reached into one of the pouches in his webbing and pulled out a cigarette and a match, running it against the striker strip. He lit his cigarette and took a long drag. The smell of the burning tobacco made Gale itch to pull his cigarettes out, but he resisted, knowing he only had so many. Charles exhaled the smoke. Gale again had to resist grabbing his own to smoke, but he held back, a monumental effort, if he did say so himself.

"What do you think we'll be doing?" Thomas asked.

"Hell if I know," Charles said, flicking ash off the end of the cigarette.

"I barely know where we are on a map," Thomas admitted. "What is this place called, Wipers?"

"Uh ... my primary school French is failing," Gale admitted.

"You're both hopeless, huh?"

"Oi, not all of us had a private tutor," Thomas gripped. "Bet Daddy dearest imported him from France and everything for you."

Charles rolled his eyes and laughed. "That was for my sister, actually. I learned Italian. Not as useful, but more fun," he continued.

"Oh, of course," Thomas said, "how could I possibly confuse that," he added, the words sounded like a dig, but it was clear that he was simply teasing.

Before the two could keep sniping at one another Sheppard returned.

"We're moving out, joining a detachment around the right flank," he said, voice clipped.

Gale and Charles shared a look. It was clear they were asking the same question: what crawled up his arse and died? The sergeant marched on without even bothering to check if they were following behind.

CHAPTER 6
October 19th-20th, 1914

None of the team had had a chance to catch a moment of sleep. By the time they had made the hike to meet with the British forces moving in on the south of Ypres from the Aisne River, it was time to advance. Gale was grateful that they didn't have to march all the way up from the river as many of the rest of the British forces. The first thing that Gale was struck by was how confusing everything seemed. There was chaos everywhere and there was no way to make sense of what was happening.

"Sarge, what are our orders?" Gale had asked as they were merging in with the BEF. The four of the Sheppard team were all walking shoulder to shoulder. It was strange to have the sergeant walking beside them instead of in front of them. Usually, Sheppard made a point of having them in a formation that made it clear he was the leader of the group. Gale wondered if he wanted to always be in front so he could make sure they knew he was willing to go into battle with them instead of behind them.

"Our orders are to check the German flank and not let them advance any further. We need to make sure our lines of communication can get shortened as much as possible between us and the isles. We're making sure to meet with the IV Corp. Rawlinson's boys," he replied. Gale had never heard of Rawlinson, but he must have been a General or something. He should have spent more time looking through the different commanders and leaders of the British military before they headed out for training after enlistment. Or at least quizzed his father on who he remembered from his time in the Boer War.

"That's it?" Gale asked.

"Yes, Private Arlington, that's it."

"Really?"

"Are you questioning the orders from high command?"

Gale shook his head, he knew if answered verbally, he would say something that he would regret. He did think that the plans were ...a bit vague. There didn't seem to be any coordinates for them to go to, or places specifically.

"Will we be on the defense, then, sir?" Thomas asked. Gale was relieved that he asked the question instead of him.

"Offense. Any other questions?"

The offense? But they were keeping the German's back. Surely, that would be mostly defensive in position.

"We know that the Germans will be advancing to Ypres and up to the coast. Our job is to make sure they're stopped, and we push them. We aren't there just to hold a position. We are there to advance it, understood?" he elaborated, answering the question that crossed Gale's mind before he could even consider asking it. He wanted to ask more, but, now, he realized why Sheppard sounded so frustrated when he left the command tent. They must have vague orders and now he was trying to find a way to make them as concrete as possible. That's why he was in line with them, wasn't it? It was strange to think about 's rank in the grand scheme of the military hierarchy, that he was in charge of training and leading his team, but he wasn't that far up compared to lieutenants and majors. Everything he was told was just pieces of the overall strategy. Gale couldn't help but wonder why the sergeant wasn't higher ranked; he was smart, competent, and a good leader. Not to mention he seemed pretty honorable to Gale. But, he was just a civilian until a few months ago. Maybe it was some sort of nuance that he didn't understand.

They continued walking until they reached the front, and before Gale even got the chance to get his barring, the fighting broke out.

The group immediately jumped into action. The fighting was much closer than Gale had gotten used to. He hadn't realized the relative luxury of having the buffer of No Man's land between him and the German troop. "Bayonet's on!" Sheppard yelled. The team quickly equipped their bayonets. Gale's stomach churned at the implications. They were going to be close enough to make the stabbing and slicing they had practiced with the bayonet more effective than shooting. His grandad's story of being in the cavalry and fighting with a saber suddenly took on a much darker light. It was still heroic, still a great story that Gale was grateful to have heard before they shipped out. But now, Gale started to realize the weight of being able to look a fellow soldier in the eye while he cut them down.

Gale shook his head, he couldn't think of the Jerries like that. They were the enemy, dead set on taking over France and then, inevitably, Britain. They were a threat to the empire, to his entire way of life. He wasn't going to let that happen. Fueled by his renewed sense of pride and patriotism, Gale pressed on, following Sheppard into the fray. As he jogged into the front line, Gale loaded his rifle, just in case. He held the rifle out and stamped down on any feelings of guilt or unease as he started to wield his bayonet. The Germans were doing the same, making it easier for Gale to fight without hesitation.

He flinched the first time he stabbed a German soldier in the stomach. He yanked the bayonet out and stabbed forward again. He could feel himself trying to shut his eyes from it. He tried not to look the soldier in the eyes—but failed. The grotesque sound of the blade cutting through fabric and piecing skin. He could feel the reverberation up the rifle as the bayonet cut against bone. He stabbed again and yanked the bayonet upward. He started to pull the bayonet out, but it had cut so deeply into the soldier's torso that it felt stuck. Gale had to pull the soldier's body closer and put his foot against the chest to get it free.

"Gale, check your six!" Charles yelled. Gale swung around, and without taking the time to aim properly, shot the soldier that was coming up behind him.

"Good looking out, mate!" Gale yelled back.

"Keep moving!" Sheppard yelled over them. Charles and Gale turned to look at him and saw the sergeant and Thomas slicing their way through the soldiers running toward them. Charles and Gale sprinted to their position and started following suit. He could feel his hands become slick with blood the longer they fought as it ran down the blade and rifle. He needed to wipe his hands or he was going to lose his grip, but there was no time. Every time he thought he would have a chance, another soldier attacked. The battle was getting far more deadly and violent than Gale had expected. The small team continued to press on. Gale saw the cavalry moving as the horses seemed huge on the battlefield, bigger than they had ever seemed in London or in the countryside back in England. As he continued to fight on, he kept the cavalry in the back of his mind. Bullets were starting to rain down from both sides. It was almost everything Gale could do to stay out of the way. It was like the cavalry had no choice. Horses were getting mowed down by the fast rate of bullets. They couldn't dodge it fast enough and they were such a big target it seemed hopeless. Then, out of nowhere there was a slight lull in the melee. Despite the relative calm in that moment, it was clear the fighting would start up again within a matter of moments. Gale had learned well, battles come in waves. They can ebb and flow; just because things slow down for a minute doesn't mean the next won't be twice as deadly.

A man on horseback rode up to them. A quick check of his uniform showed that he was a major. "Sergeant, I need to commandeer one of your men. I need someone to run this message to command, tell them what we're facing! We need them to send reinforcements."

"Private Abbey, take the message and run!" Sergeant Sheppard ordered. It made sense, Thomas was the fastest of them all in drills. That's whom Gale would have chosen too.

"Here, take this and don't stop until you can put it in the hands of command." The major handed a note to Thomas who had jogged up to him. It was a hastily written note, barely legible from the angle Gale could see. He wondered when the major had had the time to write it.

Before Thomas could ask a single question, the major rode off. Just in time, it seemed, as the fighting began in earnest again. "Go, the command will be at the back of the line!" Sheppard yelled over the sound of cannons and machine guns. Thomas nodded and started to run. Gale began to turn away to focus on the oncoming line of German soldiers when he heard a familiar yell. Gale turned again and watched as Thomas stumbled and fell to the ground. Blood was already spilling from the side of Thomas's calf. He clutched his leg, trying to stop the bleeding. The German soldiers must have seen the exchange with the major.

"Sarge!" Gale yelled, drawing Sheppard's attention as he sprinted to Thomas's side. He pulled out his field bandages and immediately began to wrap the wound. It didn't seem too deep, it should heal quickly, but at the same time, it's clear the bullet cut through the muscle. He wouldn't be able to run until it healed. Gale tightened the bandages to stop the bleeding, he didn't want to risk Thomas bleeding out. He doubted he could stave off infection; he had run out of the small amount of antiseptic that had been included in his field first-aid kit when he was treating his injury from before.

"Arlington, you take the note and run!" Sheppard yelled. Thomas was quick to hand the note over.

"I got shot in the leg, but I'm not a complete invalid yet, I can handle this, you go!" Thomas said, urging Gale on. Gale took one last look at Sheppard and Charles, they were valiantly holding the German advance back as well as they could. Other teams were coming up, forming a line of British and French soldiers in a piecemeal style. *They were going to be okay*, Gale told himself.

"Got it, I'll be fast!" Gale said. As he said that, Thomas nodded and started to load his rifle and aim at the German soldiers. His aim had been sharpened by shooting over No Man's land, just like Gale and Charles had. Gale got up and started to sprint off toward the back of the line. Gale didn't focus on the way his lungs were burning or the way his legs were protesting the longer he ran. The command center wasn't far, but after what felt like ages fighting in close range, it felt ages away. He wove himself around the fallen bodies of soldiers and horses alike. He avoided barbed wire and uneven terrain. He thought back to the conversation he had with Charles earlier about breaking his ankle.

He breathed in as his rib cage expanded to accommodate the air he was inhaling. The sounds of gunfire, cannon explosives, and yells of pain urged Gale on. He could feel sweat accumulating on his brow under his metal helmet. With each step he felt more confident he was going to make it. The small field command station was coming more and more clear as he sprinted forward. He couldn't help the smile that broke out across his face as he neared it. He started to make out the faces of the commanding officers. He schooled his expression but kept his pace up. He couldn't leave his team. The idea of his friends and sergeant fighting without him was hard for him to put up with. He knew what he was doing was urgent, he had to get this missive to the general, or whoever it was at command. They were the only ones that could call in the reinforcements that were desperately needed.

Finally, he arrived at command. He quickly saluted the men gathered around the table looking over a map. "Sirs!" he said, standing at attention. He could barely get the one word between his panting.

"Private?" The oldest-looking man said. He was definitely a general by the looks of him. Gale realized that this must be General Rawlinson.

"Message from the major, sir," Gale said, addressing the general. He held out the missive. As he did, he realized the paper had dirt and blood on it. He looked at it, hesitating to give it to the general without wiping it off, but he was worried if he did the ink would be smeared beyond recognition.

Before Gale could make a choice, General Rawlinson plucked the note from Gale's hand and read it. He looked concerned and then quickly schooled his face. "Thank you, Private ...?"

"Gale Arlington, sir, under Sergeant Allan Sheppard, sir." Gale replied.

"Very good, Private Arlington. You are dismissed."

Gale saluted and left. He didn't care if he looked silly immediately sprinting back to the line, but he had to make sure his team was still fighting. He felt responsible for them in a strange way, he wasn't a leader, that was for certain, but he knew he couldn't let them put their lives on the line without him by their side. After what felt like hours sprinting through the madness, he was finally able to reach the team and join them in the fray. He worried that the general had decided not to do anything about the missive, but as he was just losing hope that reinforcements would come, suddenly fresh French and British troops ran in. Relief filled Gale and gave him the much-needed energy boost to keep fighting. Finally, the right flank of the German army was in check. They had just managed to keep them back.

That night, Gale, Charles and Sheppard huddle around a small fire. While they weren't directly on the front, having moved back when reinforcements arrived, they were close enough that if the flames got too big, they would give away their location to the enemy. Thomas had been taken to the small field hospital to ensure his leg didn't get infected. He was going to go back to the Marne early because of it. Gale had to admit he was a bit relieved by that news. The trio was eating their rations in relative quiet. This time their meal came in a can. Gale tried not to think too hard about what it was he was eating. He had realized over the past couple months the more he thought about it the more nauseated he felt. It wasn't worth it to contemplate the strange, grayish-pink preserved meat that he was eating too much. How he missed Mrs. Carson's Scotch eggs.

Sheppard had just returned from command, and it seemed like he had something to say to them. He had been called away about an hour earlier by a major that Gale was certain he saw at the command tent. The two men spoke in hushed whispers before they both left. Gale and Charles had speculated about what they could be talking about. Part of Gale worried that something had happened to Thomas or the team back in the Marne. He had shaken that particular thought out of his head. Arthur was a good leader; he'd been taking care of his brothers since before he could spell. They were going to be fine. Thomas was fine, like he had said earlier, it was just a graze, nothing serious, just bad enough he couldn't run on it. He had even managed to limp away from the field, not requiring to be carried by a stretcher. Although, Gale wasn't sure if he did it out of a sense of pride more than a genuine ability. But, who was he to judge? He was certain if the roles were flipped he would have done the same.

Sheppard took a deep breath, immediately pulling Gale and Charles out of their own respective thoughts. "We did a good job today, lads. Gale, you did enough to impress the general. You should be proud of yourself, both of you."

"Thank you, sir," Gale and Charles said.

"We did such a good job that we've been given another mission. I want you both to know I will not think any less of you if you decide not to go on it. It'll be dangerous, and it's nothing that I have trained you in."

"What is it, sir?" Gale asked, unable to stop himself. The curiosity was already gnawing away at his decorum.

"They want us to go to the enemy camp," Sheppard said.

"What?" Charles asked, he looked incredulous. "They can't be serious, sir."

"But they are Private Dunford. They believe the Germans are planning something, but they need reconnaissance. They thought since our team was able to deliver that missive from the front we were the best candidates on hand to do this. They don't have any scouts available."

"It'll be dangerous," Gale said, saying what the other two were clearly thinking.

"Very, if we get caught, we could be killed or taken prisoner," Sheppard said. "Given that we would be working in an intelligence-gathering capacity, execution would be the kinder. As I said, I will not think less of you two if either of you decide not to go. You weren't trained in this and didn't sign up for it."

"I'll go," Gale said, he didn't even need to consider it. It was his duty to go. "I did sign up for it. Anything for King and Country, right?"

Sheppard nodded. "Right. Dunford?"

Charles's lips pressed tightly together as he thought about. It was clear he was hesitant.

"Like I said, Private, there's not punishment if you choose not to—"

"I'll go. Can't let that one go too long without supervision. His dad and grandad would kill me, sir," Charles said, elbowing Gale.

"Great. Leave your things. Take only your bayonets. I'll have my pistol as well, in case we get into a skirmish. We can't afford the rifles shooting off and giving us away," Sheppard instructed.

"What, we're going now?" Charles asked.

"Did you expect we'd pop over at teatime, Private?" Sheppard asked.

Gale couldn't help but snicker at the thought. It earned him a sharp look from Charles that he easily shrugged off.

They took off their webbing, leaving most of their things behind as they were told by their sergeant and the group quickly started to sneak off. There was a forest that flanked the battlefield. They made a beeline for the tree line. It would help to hide their approach and sounds coming from a forest wouldn't be completely unexpected from any waiting guards.

"Let's hope we don't meet the Big Bad Wolf," Charles whispered. Gale hummed in agreement. That would be the last thing they needed to run into at that moment.

As they neared the camp edge of the German camp, Sheppard raised up his hand, signaling for Gale and Charles to stop and be quiet. Gale could just make out the silhouettes of the patrol walking by. Sheppard turned and nodded for them to move further back. The three treaded carefully further into the forest, avoiding any sticks they could make out by the light of the moon. Gale shuddered as he stepped on a particularly loud crinkled leaf. Fall had hit Belgium and

France hard, the forest floor was covered in what had made up the tree's canopy. The underbrush was dried out and dead, making sneaking around particularly difficult. They could shuffle through it because it would create the loud sound of shifted leaves. Instead, they had to tread as lightly as possible and do their best to avoid large piled-up sections of underbrush mixed with starved leaves.

"We need to watch and time the patrol. That way we can know how much time we have to get in and out of the camp. We'll move together. Arlington, you'll be in charge of getting the intelligence from the command tent. Charles and I will keep guard and watch your back. Understand?"

"Yes, sir," Gale and Charles said. It was a lot of responsibility, and suddenly Gale wished that he had paid far more attention to Finn when he was tutoring him in German than he did. But it wasn't the time for regrets. Rather, he needed to focus. Sheppard pulled out a familiar stopwatch, the one from training, Gale realized, and signaled for them to move back to the edge of the tree line. The guards came around again, and Sheppard started his timer. The three stood stalk still, all equally on edge as they waited for the guards to return. Three minutes passed until the patrol came back around. One guard looked out toward the trees. The three stepped back in unison, all holding their breath as the German guard seemed to lean forward and squinted his eyes like he was trying to verify if he had seen something at all. But, after a moment, he seemed to have decided that he did not, indeed, see anything.

His fellow guard asked him a question, but since Gale's German was almost as bad as his French, he had no idea what was asked. Maybe he was wondering what was bothering the other guard. The guard that had looked into the forest waved his partner off and they continued on their cycle of patrol. As they rounded the corner of the far side of the camp, Sheppard signaled them to move out. The trio silently snuck into the camp. Most soldiers seemed to be asleep, aside from the patrolling guards. Regardless, they were careful when they were about to head down a makeshift path that had an obscured view from them, looking around corners. They all had their knives drawn.

Sheppard had his pistol; he used it as he led them to the center of the camp.

Gale knew the second they had reached the command tent. It was bigger and taller than the rest of the tents. Big enough to have an office and a sleeping area. It was then it dawned on Gale that someone might be in the tent when he snuck in. He looked at Sheppard and wanted to voice this concern, but the sergeant pressed a finger to his lips, reminding Gale that it was not the time to speak. They slowly snuck up to the tent and looked around. There was no sound or movement indicating they had been seen. Before he could hesitate any longer, Gale slid into the tent. His worst fear was immediately confirmed as stepped inside.

He could hear gentle snoring. *Just what I needed*, he thought. However, he was lucky in that a small gas lamp was still burning, flame flickering, threatening to go out any second, but it would be enough for him to quickly scan documents to see if they would be helpful.

Gale tip-toed up to the desk, trying to avoid making any unnecessary noise. His gaze was fixed on the outline of the sleeping form on the cot. He tracked the breathing, making sure it stayed slow and deep, no indications of anyone awakened. Gale held his breath, not trusting himself to breathe quietly enough to avoid alerting the sleeping man to his presence. His documents lined the desk. Gale was partly elated and partly concerned. There was no way he could possibly read them all to find the important elements. He could just take all of them, he thought. It wasn't like he couldn't leave evidence behind that he stole them. They were, after all, at war. Then again, he didn't want to take anything that wasn't necessary. What if he brought back personal letters or missives about laundry that had no place in being brought back to the British and French generals? He settled for quickly scanning the top few documents, hoping they would have words that he recognized that would also be relevant.

Quickly he identified something: *eine falle*. A trap. He scanned the rest of the text until he saw other words that seemed important. *Die küste*, the coast. And finally *flanke*. Flank. Gale wasn't sure what it meant, but anything with the words trap, coast, and flank seemed important to him. He grabbed the top five pages, prayed to God it was enough, and quickly stole out of the tent. Charles and Sheppard were right where they had left them, standing outside the tent on guard. He held up the pages to Sheppard and then folded them up and shoved them into his shirt. He was not going to lose them. Sheppard and Charles smiled, they were certainly going to celebrate when they got back and delivered the necessary documents.

Sheppard let them out the same way they came in and the team made quick work of returning back to camp. They made a beeline to command, the tent flaps were open and warm light spilled out. The general was waiting for them. Sheppard clapped Gale on the back. "You go in first, Arlington."

"You sure?"

"You did all the hard work, Gale, of course he's sure," Charles said, answering for the sergeant.

"I concur. Go ahead, Private."

Gale nodded and stepped into the command tent after a beat Sheppard and Charles followed him in. He was greeted with the sight of General Rawlinson and his lieutenant colonels leaning over a map. Gale cleared his throat, trying to get their attention in the least intrusive way. Their heads snapped up immediately.

"Ah, Private Arlington. Wonderful to see you again. Have you brought back the intel requested?" the general asked. He sounded tired, understandably given the late hour. Gale knew he normally would have but the adrenaline pumping through his body made it impossible for him to even consider the thought of sleeping at the moment.

"Yes, sir," Gale said, he reached into his shirt and pulled out the folded up pages. "I believe there is a trap that's being set, sir," Gale said. He handed the pages over to the general.

"Is that so?" the general said, already looking more alert.

"Yes sir, my German isn't great, but I saw the words *eine falle*."

"Very good, I'm glad there was much less bloodshed involved in this recovery," General Rawlinson said lightly.

"Me too, sir," Gale said, unsure of what else could be said.

"Right, well, thank you all for your work tonight. I know it couldn't have been easy. I'll be sure to send word of your bravery back to HQ. Dismissed." With that the trio left and returned to their camp. Gale could only hope that the intelligence he gathered would be able to help them in the coming days.

CHAPTER 7

November 21st-30th, 1914

In the morning, after Gale had gathered the intelligence, news spread through the front line that they were to start heading west, along the coast. The change in orders came as a shock to many of the soldiers, but Sheppard, Gale, and Charles all had knowing looks. They knew why. The intelligence they had managed to retrieve was worthwhile and mattered enough to change the strategy. They had ordered and had gotten into quite a few skirmishes with the Germans. The French and British fought back against the Germans. At times it was impossible to tell who was actually winning. The lines kept moving back and forth as both sides were desperate to outflank each other. Even though Gale had been optimistic at first that they were going to be able to pull ahead and win with the information he had managed to steal, it seemed there were more consequences to his theft than originally thought. The German's must have quickly figured out that their enemy knew their strategy. They must have changed their movements to accommodate the intelligence leak. Gale again cursed his lack of linguistic skills—if he had just been able to read the letters, he could have taken down notes and delivered those instead of stealing the documents themselves.

A couple days passed and the battle for Ypres and the sea seemed to drag on. More and more soldiers died. The trio were exhausted, they had been fighting for three days straight, and it was clear they needed to be relieved. The fighting itself flagged. They must not be the only ones feeling that way. Gale realized as the battles waned, they were no less intense than they were at the beginning. Instead, it was the exhaustion pulling at every soldiers' movements that made it feel so. Surely the higher-ups had noticed. It was a grueling marathon of battles. Gale found himself growing numb to the smell of decaying bodies and the sight of grotesque injuries. He had even gotten used to searching the dead for extra supplies of bullets, rations, and bandages just to keep on him, just in case. Gale, Charles, and Sheppard were all three lucky; they hadn't been injured badly, but they had all been sliced a few times by bayonet blades and stray barbed wire.

Gale had lost track of where they were geographically. He couldn't be sure if they were in France or Belgium on any given day. Despite all the battles and skirmishes, the regiment they were traveling with pressed onward. He was able to tell they were moving Northwest, up to the coastline. He could only hope this push would result in them getting close enough to the coast to secure the ports through the English Channel. If they did that, then everything would be worth it. One day, as the regiment marched onward, Gale began to smell the familiar saltwater scent of the ocean. They passed through a town, and that's when Gale realized where they were. They were in Dunkirk. In France. Right on the English Channel. They had done it.

Amazement washed over Gale just as quickly as the sense of relief. He couldn't believe that they had managed to fight and trek their way from just the grounds of Ypres all the way over to Dunkirk and live. "We're in Dunkirk," he said, in daze.

"That we are, Gale," Charles said, in the same sort of daze.

"We made it to the channel."

"That we did."

Neither of them could quite believe that they had done it.

Sheppard walked up behind them. "You've done great work, lads. This battle is over for us."

"What do you mean, sir?" Gale asked.

"We got new orders, we're heading back to Fiddler's Crossing. In a train, if you can believe it," Sheppard elaborated. If Gale were honest, he couldn't believe it at all, actually. The battle wasn't done. Nothing had been decided. There was no victor.

"But, if we leave now, aren't we abandoning ... all of this?" Gale asked, gesturing outward toward the rest of the troops and back toward Ypres.

"No, we're not. Our team is mobile. We go where we are needed and right now, there's a lull in fighting, it's a good time for us to be relieved of duty here. I'm tired, you're tired. Our fighting is getting sloppy and that's dangerous. I spoke with the generals, and it's time for us to head back. Need to make sure our trench is still standing, yeah?"

Gale nodded; that made sense. He looked to Charles, who seemed equally satisfied by the explanation.

Just like Sheppard had promised, they got to take a train. Only, it was a cargo train. There were no seats. Just an empty car that was quickly filled with soldiers heading back to the Marne. It was clear the generals had decided to rotate out the troops after the sergeant had suggested they let him and his team head back. As Gale sat in the train and observed the other soldiers, he could understand why command had taken Sheppard's request and run with it. They all seemed completely worn out. They were covered in dirt and dry bits of blood and other bodily matter that Gale decided he didn't want to consider. As he looked at them, all leaning against the rumbling walls of the train car, Gale realized that he probably looked exactly like them. Tired, wrung out, filthy. In need of some rest and proper food.

"Hey, Charles?" Gale said, nudging his half-asleep friend.

"Yeah?" Charles said, barely coherent.

"Think they managed to get a kitchen set up in the trenches?"

At that question, Charles' stomach growled loudly. "God, I hope so. I refuse to eat anymore of that canned ... substance," Charles said, finally settling on a word to describe the rations after a beat of searching for one that would fit it. "Do you think if we wrote Mrs. Carson, asking for them, that she would be able to mail us her Scotch eggs and that they'd arrive before they were spoiled?" Charles asked.

"Oh, I wish she could. That sounds bloody brilliant right now."

"Mmm ... or maybe one of her steak pies ..." Charles mused.

"I'd even go for the curry at the gentlemen's club right now," Gale commiserated.

"Oi, you two," a half asleep Sheppard said, "knock it off with all that talk of food, we're all hungry, no need to make it worse."

"Sorry, sir," Gale said. He leaned back against the wooden wall of the train car and hoped he wouldn't get a splinter in the back of the neck. That would be all he needed, death by splinter infection after surviving that battle. He laughed at the idea.

"What's so funny?" Charles asked, words slurring from exhaustion.

"Nothing. Just ...thought about another thing to add to the list of dumb ways to die at war that wouldn't be in battle."

"Ah, what is it this time?"

"Death by splinter infection or sepsis."

"Splinter sepsis, huh? That would be godawful. And humiliating. Hey, Sarge, how would you write home about that?" Charles asked.

The sergeant never answered that question; he was already fast asleep. Gale studied his face for a beat and realized that he really wasn't nearly as old as Gale had originally assumed or what he guessed before they shipped out. The mustache and war-weary expression he had seemed to age him when he was awake. Asleep, he looked like he could be the McGuinnesses' long-lost oldest brother. He looked pretty similar to Arthur, and when he was tired or not talking in an official capacity, he spoke using the same terms and slang, too. He wondered if he grew up anywhere near them. Gale let his mind wander as he allowed his eyes to slide shut and for the darkness of sleep to take him.

The arrival back to Fiddler's Crossing was both more and less exciting than he thought. The second the trio showed their faces in the trench they were greeted with loud whoops of excitement.

"You made it!" Thomas yelled.

"Good to have you back," Finn added.

"Finally," Rory chimed in.

Arthur waved from his spot manning the machine gun. "Nice to see you're back!"

"Yeah, good to know Thomas didn't just leave you lot for dead," Barry said, laughing. His humor was sorely missed as all three of them began to laugh heartily.

"Christ, you're gone for a month and you come back thinking I'm hilarious—you should head off on secret missions more often," Barry continued.

"You have no idea," Gale said. The group quickly got stuck in as Gale regaled them with the stories from Ypres.

"Wow, so you're a proper spy now, huh?" Rory asked, excitement gleaming in his eyes.

"I wouldn't go that far. I stole the pages—that's how the Germans knew that we knew what they were up to," Gale admitted, the weight of the guilt still resting on his shoulders. *How many more soldiers died because of that*, he wondered to himself.

"Hey, if you hadn't done that, who knows what would have happened," Charles said. "Besides, you barely speak a lick of German but you were still able to pick out the right documents. That's far better than I would have done."

"Arlington, you did good, the fight up there was always going to be bloody. There was a lot at stake. Accept that you did all you could, and you are a hero for it," Sheppard said. "That's an order," he tacked on.

"Ah, fine," Gale said reluctantly. He wasn't exactly comfortable being called a hero. Following orders seemed like a very low bar for him to cross to be called a hero. "Enough about Ypres, what happened here?"

Rory immediately seized the opportunity to tell Gale, Charles, and Sheppard, about the hijinks he and Barry had gotten into. And how a proper kitchen got set up. "Or should I call it a mess, because that place is a disgrace to all kitchens. It's just a big pot filled with water and rations. But, yesterday, Finn got a carrot. First vegetable I've seen since we reached the trench," Rory said, laughing. "He wouldn't even share it with us."

"You've never liked cooked carrots, why would you start now?" Finn said as a way of justification.

"I've been to war, now," Rory started. "I'm a changed man, all of me is different for it. Maybe I like them now. Have you considered that?"

"Oh, you're so right, my apologies for not considering the grand changes you've been through," Finn replied, rolling his eyes.

"*Ah, bonjour, mon amis!*" a man called.

"Hello, Jean," Arthur called back. A Frenchman walked down the corridor of the trenches and was quickly in sight. He had dark hair and dark eyes and was of average height and build. Nothing really stood out to Gale about his outward appearance, but he seemed friendly enough.

"Who are you?" Sheppard asked, his words were clipped, but his tone was not unkind.

"Ah, my apologies, *monsieur*. I am Jean Valois, a member of the French Artillery. I man one of the cannons set up along the line here," he explained.

His English is excellent, Gale thought.

"You must be the sergeant of Fiddler's Cross, *oui*?"

"Yes, Sergeant Sheppard."

"A pleasure. Well, I am here to steal your men's cigarettes once more." Jean pulled out a set of playing cards. "Would any of you three care to join?"

As it turned out Jean was not lying when he said he was going to take their cigarettes. Round after round of cards he managed to trump all of them.

"What can I say, I am gifted," Jean laughed.

"Ugh, I fold," Charles said, tossing his cards into the middle. "I'm going to need these to get over the losses," he added, patting his cigarette case.

"Same here," Gale agreed. Despite them all losing to the

Frenchmen over and over again, the Sheppard team got along with him easily, and Gale was grateful to have made a new friend in him.

The next days all pass in relative peace and quiet for the front lines. Gale quickly discovered that Rory was right, the kitchen was barely even a kitchen, it was a mess in both senses of the words. But the cabbage that seemed to make up most of the soup they got from the kitchen made it worth it. It seemed that as the days got colder and longer, the British and French armies had decided to close ranks with each other and share rations and supplies more fully. That included their trenches. *It probably made communication between everyone much easier*, Gale thought. The mail system was set up, and they met Peter Connelly, the mailman of the trenches, he called himself. He had been apparently making a complete map of the trenches and writing out the different names of each section.

"Makes my job that much easier," he had said, showing off his map. It was very complete, and Gale realized just how large and complex the trench system had gotten. "I've heard from higher-ups that the trenches will be here to stay, so you might want to make yourselves comfortable," Peter had said one day on his delivery run.

"Really?"

"Yeah, seems like that battle up in Ypres cemented it. Now that the weather is getting much colder now as winter is setting it, I think it'd be worth it," Peter explained. Gale agreed, getting some sort of insulation from the cold weather in the sleeping dugout would be nice, although he doubted they would be able to find too much material to help with that.

Gale was quickly proven wrong. Once he had talked to Sheppard about Peter's prediction, quickly refocused most of the team's tasks back on building up Fiddler's Crossing. They got more sandbags and used them to line the floor of the dugout, creating a barrier between them and the mud that now laid beneath. They also grabbed more wood and spent time bulking up the wall and floors of the trench outside of the dugout. The whole area felt more like an actual building or home really now that they had taken the time to renovate Fiddler's

Crossing from when it was first built. If nothing else, it was a lot more comfortable for the quickly onsetting winter. Gale couldn't help but be impressed with the work they had all done—even if he didn't want to really believe they were going to be there much longer. He kept reminding himself of the promised home by Christmas, unwilling to admit to himself that things were unlikely to be done by then.

Seemingly satisfied with all of the renovations they did to the trench, Sheppard decided it was time to touch up the skills they'd learned in training. "You have to keep sharp, lads. Just because it's been quiet doesn't mean that things can't start up again at a moment's notice," he had said. Most of the drilling was about speeding up the time it took them to load and reload the gun and about using the bayonet. Gale still hadn't been able to clean all the blood off of his, so each time he brandished it he was reminded of what it felt like to use it. The blade felt much heavier in his hand now than it had ever felt before he went to Ypres. He could clearly see the stunned eyes of the first German soldier he had killed with it. He could feel the heat of the blood pooling over the blade and running over his hand. Gale tried to block all of that out of his mind as Sheppard made them work on their stabbing technique over and over again. Gale supposed he was worried about what would happen if they got into close-range combat again if the rest of the team was as unprepared as they were at the beginning of the battle in Belgium.

"You'd think he'd be happy knowing we've survived this long with only one casualty," Charles had muttered to Gale. "Jean told me about how they lost half their team in a single day. We all must be doing something right, right?"

"I think he took Michael's ... well, I think he took it personally," Gale replied. "Like it was his fault he didn't train him enough or something."

"Maybe, but ...after all we did in Belgium, you'd think it would be enough to prove that we're not ill prepared."

Gale hummed in agreement. Sheppard had turned to look at them with a quizzical look, but Gale didn't want him to question them about what they had been discussing. That would be beyond unideal.

That night, after hours of rigorous training, the team finally sat down around a fire, letting themselves bask in its warmth. They were eating their rations for the night and were laughing and telling stories. If they didn't all have a rifle by their side and metal helmets on, Gale could have almost believed that it was a group of men on a camping trip. Or that they were a bunch of overgrown boy scouts. Not that they were at war with a rival country intent on spreading its empire. As it were, it was the kind of night that Gale knew he would treasure as he aged. Something to remind him of the humanity behind the fight. He wondered if his dad and grandad had the same sort of memories, or if they became too painful to consider after they had lost their friends? Gale could only hope that didn't happen to him.

The group had been telling stories of what it was like growing up where they are from. Most of them were from London. Gale was amazed that he hadn't met Barry before the war, his family had a large flat in Kensington, paid for by their jewelry store. Apparently, his father specialized in silversmithing. Which sounded like a fascinating job. "What about you Sarge?" Gale asked when they reached a lull in the conversation. "Where did you grow up?"

"London, near Bethnal Green Junction," Sheppard said. He said it with a cool tone, as if he was challenging any of them to say anything. Bethnal Green Junction was not an affluent area of London to say the least. Rather, it was in the East End. What set it apart from the rest of the area was the number of workshops that were there. "My family are tailors, by trade," he added.

"We grew up 'round there, didn't we boys?" Arthur said.

"We moved a few years ago, our dad is a clerk, like Arthur," Finn added.

Sheppard's guard seemed to come down a bit at that comment. Gale understood why he was standoffish about it, though. People that were more privileged like him, Charles, and Barry were known to be judgmental about where people were born in London, what district was just as important as what accent you spoke with.

"My great-grandparents lived there too, a long time ago," Barry said. "Weren't anywhere else for them to live, really. Being Jewish and all. They were lucky they were so skilled, it helped them get out."

"Right," Sheppard said, "my family just liked it there. They had a real community that they didn't want to turn their backs on," Sheppard said, then looked away, like his mind just caught up with his mouth. "I meant ..."

"No worries, I get what you mean," Barry said.

The group sat in an uneasy silence until Gale popped up and asked "Why did you join the military?"

"I wanted to see the world. All the British Empire," Sheppard said. "And, at the time, I thought I could rise through the ranks quickly," he admitted.

"When did you enlist?" Charles asked.

"End of 1902, when I was nineteen, seemed like a better bet than tailoring, and I was posted in India and Egypt for a while. Then, I made sergeant and stayed a sergeant, which didn't bother me over there. Things were more, casual, as a member of the British Army over there. And then, I was sent back to England just in time for the war to start. Now I'm here." Gale nodded, he was in the military for just over ten years, he was thirty-one. Much younger than Gale had thought.

"Wow, what was India like?" Thomas asked. "I hadn't even left London before I enlisted. It must have been amazing.

"It was ... it was good. I miss it there." Gale had a feeling that when Sheppard was talking about India he was really talking about someone.

"Is there someone there missing you?" Finn asked, Gale realized he was not the only one picking up on that.

Sheppard nodded. "Leela, my wife. I hope to return to her soon. She was pregnant when I left. I want to meet my child."

"I understand that," Thomas said, "My wife, Mary, sent me a portrait of my son, Ollie. He looks so much bigger already," Thomas's tone was melancholic, mirroring Sheppard's. Gale was amazed that they were both so willing to stay in this war, having someone that depended on them waiting for them. Gale knew that he was lucky, his main reason for fighting in the war was to defend Britain and become a man. To live up to his father and grandfather's expectations. It was his duty. But Sheppard and Thomas had duties to their family too. It was strange to think about it. He never would have guessed that Sheppard had someone at home, he was so professional.

The group stayed huddled together as a cold wind cut through the trenches. Gale and the others all were grateful that they had a fire to keep warm. Gale could only wonder what it would be like when fall ended, and winter well and truly began. As he leaned in to warm his hand up, again, Gale sent a small prayer to God that the war would end soon and he wouldn't have to find out.

CHAPTER 8

December 24th-25th, 1914

Snow was falling from the sky, compounding on top of the icy slush that was already covering the ground. Gale tightened his jacket around himself as he trudged his way back from his posting at the machine gun. Arthur had come to relieve him just in time for him to make sure his fingers didn't freeze and fall off. Even though Gale had wool knit gloves that his mother had sent along a few weeks ago, they did very little to keep out the wet chill of winter. Not to mention that they already had a small hole in them where the thumb was joined to the rest of the glove from when Gale had been cleaning his rifle. He was grateful that the gaiters that covered his boots and cuffs of his thick wool pants kept the slush at bay.

Gale's nose and cheeks were bright red and wind chapped. But it was nothing new at this point. Luckily the dugouts were dry even if they were not the warmest. The group had gotten used to sleeping in shifts to stay on the lookout and be aware of any movement over No Man's land. Doing so allowed them to share blankets to keep warm while they slept. It was just before midnight on Christmas Eve, and he desperately wanted to sleep. Gale watched as cigarette smoke floated out of the dugout opening. *Charles must be there*, he thought. The smoke added to the gray haze of the winter sky and atmosphere. The pale moon was blocked by thick clouds threatening a long day of snow. As a child, Gale had always hoped for a white Christmas. To him, nothing was more magical than leaving the Christmas Eve Midnight Mass to see large, fluffy, snowflakes falling from the velvety black sky. Or to run outside Christmas morning and see a large blanket of snow covering the world around him. It had always made him so certain that St. Nick had visited. As he grew up, that magical element had faded, but he still loved the look of snow on the ground, frost creeping up his window creating intricate patterns that he'd trace late at night when he couldn't sleep, and ice covering branches of trees in a glossy glaze. When he had a home or dorm to run inside to, winter was his favorite season. He loved being around his friends and family. Throwing snowballs and then running in for mulled wine and a mince pie. But, in the trench, he did have to admit that he was starting to see the downsides of the season.

As he entered the dugout, his eyes took a couple seconds to adjust to the relative darkness. There was a single gas lamp that illuminated the sleeping area. The dugout had quickly become the place for the team to hang out when they weren't on duty. Charles, Barry, Finn, and Jean were all sitting in a circle playing cards. They were all smoking; it was a habit that helped soothe their nerves and pass time. They always had something to do as long as they had a cigarette to smoke. Gale was personally longing for the smooth taste and smoke that came from the cigars his granddad had. He had mentioned them in his last letter home hoping that maybe he'd get one as a Christmas gift. Unfortunately, Peter had told them that it was unlikely they were getting any more mail until after Boxing Day. Gale supposed that he couldn't complain, really. He should be grateful that he was still in one piece and that he hadn't really been injured since the first day of the Battle of the Marne.

"You alright, mate?" Barry asked.

"Yeah," Gale replied. He took off his gloves and shook them off. He put them next to the gas lamp in a vain effort to dry them. He had done this every day since the first serious snow back in the beginning of December, but it had never been fully successful. But, any attempt at getting them more dry than they currently were was a win in his books. Gale shook a bit to knock any of the snow that had stuck to his wool jacket off and then grabbed one of the folded blankets and wrapped it tightly around himself and joined the others. He knew that he'd get a chance to catch up on sleep in a bit, after all, the next day was Christmas, and he couldn't fathom the idea of a battle breaking out on one of the biggest holy days in the Christian calendar. Surely even the Germans would respect that.

Just as they settled into a new round of cards he started to hear Arthur shouting. "Guys! Get out here! Hurry!" Gale and the rest of the boys in the dugout tossed their blankets to the side, grabbed their rifles and sprinted to their rendezvous point near the machine gun. As they ran through the corridors of the trench to meet with the rest of the team, Gale was struck with the distinct lack of gun and artillery fire. It was quiet. The loudest noise was the sounds of soldiers' webbing vests smacking against their backs with each stride. Then they made it to Arthur, Rory, Thomas, and Sheppard's location.

Gale immediately climbed to the top of the trench, pointing his rifle out. Charles and Barry followed suit without hesitating. Then, as they peered across No Man's land they realized that there was no danger. Gale turned to look at Arthur. "What's wrong?"

"They were singing, just ... just listen!" Arthur said, voice hushed. Just as the eldest McGuinness finished his sentence, Gale could hear a large choir of voices singing the chorus of Silent Night in German. It seemed to echo all the way across No Man's land. Gale couldn't help but hum along with them. He then looked around and saw other soldiers slowly climbing out of their dugouts as they heard the Christmas carol. One moment the Allies' soldiers were listening in wonder and the next they were joining in. It was a moment that seemed to transcend language. Warmth bloomed across Gale's chest. He took a deep breath and joined in with the rest of his team. He shouldered his rifle and climbed off the parapet. It felt strangely miraculous as the two sides formed a mass choir of military carolers. A peaceful camaraderie seemed to ripple throughout the whole valley. Charles leaned over and whispered into Gale's ear.

"Maybe the War Office was on to something when they said the war would be over by Christmas," he said.

Gale nodded, "Just a few days off," Gale commented.

"That's the government for you, always expect a delay unless they're collecting taxes."

The two laughed lightheartedly for the first time in months. As the two childhood friends rejoined the carolers, Gale felt a smile break across his face. In that moment, he knew, no matter what, things were going to be okay.

The night faded into dawn as the two sides continued to sing classic carols. By the time the morning sun had risen, Gale found himself amazed at the evening events. He had thought that would be the end of it. All of the Sheppard team filled back into the dugout to get some sleep. Who knew how long the peace would actually last. After what felt like a matter of minutes a loud siren started blaring. It was an alert to come up the trenches, ready to avoid an attack. The siren was loud and disconcerting on purpose. There was no way to mistake it for anything but what it was, a warning.

Confusion and worry riddled their way through Gale. His heart was pounding in fear for the second time that night. He and the rest of the team got up and sprinted out of the dugout. They carried their rifles. How could things change so quickly? Less than an hour ago they had been singing carols together, were they going to be fighting in earnest.

"Can't the Huns let us have anything?" Rory gripped as he climbed up the trench next to Gale.

"Who knows!" Gale replied. As they stepped up and rested their rifles on the parapet. Then, Gale saw a figure climb up and out of the German trench. Gale leaned forward and squinted. "Is he ...?"

"Waving a white flag?" Sheppard finished. He seemed to be just as confused as the rest of the team.

"Is that a commanding officer?" Charles asked.

"His uniform says he is," Finn said, looking through the one pair of binoculars they had.

"Give that here," Sheppard said, holding out his hand, waiting for

Finn to place the binoculars into his hand. Finn did so and Sheppard used them to look out.

Then, before anyone could say anything else, the sirens stopped. The whole valley descended into complete silence for the first time in months. The only noise was the hollow sound of the wind. A few moments passed. Gale wondered what was going to happen. He didn't want to trust the white flag.

"It's a trap, right?" Rory whispered, hesitant to break the silence for once.

"I ... I don't know," Sheppard admitted.

Stopping the team in their tracks before they could spend any more time speculating, more and more German soldiers followed the officer out. None of them were carrying any weapons. Instead, they all appeared to be holding small parcels wrapped in fabric. What were they? Gale wondered. It was a heady sight to watch so many soldiers appear out of the trench. Were there always that many less than a couple dozen yards away?

The officer continued forward through No Man's land until he reached the halfway point. Gale held his breath scared about what could happen next. The show of trust the officer was performing was beyond admirable. What if someone shot him right then? Would a battle break out? Would the Allies use their machine guns to gun down all the German soldiers standing above the trenches?

The German officer set his shoulders and took a deep breath. "Let us not fight today!" he proclaimed, German accent thick. "Today, let us be friends!" The officer smiled.

After a beat, a British officer climbed out of the trench. In his hand he holds out what looked to be a silver cigarette case. A gift, Gale realized. The British officer walked out into No Man's land to meet the German officer halfway. Gale swallowed. He couldn't help but worry about what could happen next. He thought about the German soldiers he had fought and killed. He thought about Michael falling to the ground, his blood mixing with the dirt. Worry riddled its way into his heart, his blood rushed through his ears and his pulse raced. Then, he watched as the two officers shook hands. The British officer turned around and waved at the allied soldiers, making the gesture for them to come forward.

"Today will be a day of peace! A truce!" The officer yelled, a smile that matched the German officer's spread across his face.

Giddy excitement bubbled throughout Gale. A Christmas truce. Gale turned to Sheppard, waiting for 's permission to move.

"You heard the officer, let's go," Sheppard said, he seemed to be just as excited at the prospect of a truce with the German's for the day.

"So this is a Christmas miracle, huh?" Barry said, laughing. The team all climbed up and over the trench wall. Gale reached into his pocket and pulled out his own cigarette case. As the team moved through No Man's land, the eeriness that had always marked the space between the two sides faded away. Once they reached the middle, they were all quickly greeted by a bunch of German soldiers.

With Finn translating for the team, they were able to muddle through the language barrier. A few of the German soldiers spoke English as well, making it even easier to communicate.

Soon a football game broke out between the two sides. They used the broken pieces of wood to indicate the goalposts. Arthur and Charles joined the Allied offense positions. Both used their natural athleticism to score a couple goals for the British. Gale played defense and managed to steal the ball from one of the German soldiers. He passed to Charles, who kicked it to a French soldier he had never met before. A feeling of warmth and joy seemed to hang in the air. The football game ended in a well-earned tie. The group split up, and Gale quickly found himself and his team in the middle of a gift exchange. Sheppard had asked Barry and Rory to go back to their dugout and grab the box that was shoved under his cot. When they returned, Sheppard revealed that he had a bottle of whiskey and a Christmas pudding to share with a small team of German soldiers. They all sat around and celebrated the holiday that begged merriness from all.

"It is nice, no? That we can be friends for a day?" One of the soldiers, a man named Franz, mused.

"That it is, Franz," Charles said. He took a swig of Sheppard's whiskey and passed the bottle to Franz.

"This is good. I will be sad when I won't get it again," Franz said, holding up the bottle.

The group laughed, "Yes, I agree," another German soldier said, "Our lager is good, but is nothing like this."

"You can thank the Irish," Sheppard said. "My gran sent it along a month ago."

"God bless the Irish," Franz said. Then he pulled out a cigar. He cut the tip with a knife in his pocket and lit it. He took a puff, making sure the flame took. "Here, this we can share." The group continued to laugh with one another sharing their holiday traditions. Slowly, the sun began to set and the group realized it was time to return to their respective trenches. As they started to part ways, Franz turned back to them.

"I promise I will not shoot you, if I come across you in battle," Franz said, crossing his heart. A smile pulled at the corner of his mouth, despite the humor in his tone he was sincere.

"We'll do the same, then!" Sheppard called back.

The group parted ways, returning to their own sides. The Christmas truce was a show of chivalry that proved to Gale there was still honor in war and that someday soon both sides would come to agreeable terms and things would return to normal. Maybe they weren't home for Christmas this year, but Gale knew that by next year they would be.

CHAPTER 9

January 1st-8th, 1915

The status quo quickly returned to the trenches. The constant sound of the gunfire returned as well as the intensity of manning the machine gun and keeping lookout for the men controlling the bigger gun. The only time that Gale felt calm was when the group sat together and had dinner together. It also happened to be the only time that the whole team had time to be together. Nowadays it often felt like Sheppard's team had been split in half. Gale, Finn, Barry, and Arthur made up the night shift, and Rory, Thomas and Charles were the day shift alongside Sheppard.

Gale was starting to worry a bit about Sheppard, after all, he would come up during the night shift and keep looking out with Gale and Finn for hours at a time. *Did the man ever sleep?* Gale wondered one morning as he headed back to the dugout. He had just seen Sheppard barely an hour ago and now the sergeant had just relieved the night shift of their duties so they could go get some food and rest. The group were just about to duck into the dugout when they saw two men followed by a group of lieutenants marching angrily down the trench right toward them. One of the men was a French general, the other was a British general. Gale immediately recognized both of them. It was General Ferdinand Foch and General Douglas Haig. Both men looked like they were in their sixties, had mustaches that curled up the sides, gray hair, and expressions that were so sour they could spoil milk.

Before any of the night shift team could stand at attention and salute, General Haig lifted up his hand and pointed directly at Gale. "You, there, Private, where is your sergeant?"

"Up on the parapet by our machine gun, sir," Gale replied, immediately.

"Good, take us to him, the rest of you come too." Haig's tone was so no-nonsense that Gale immediately took off toward where Sheppard and the rest of the team were. Gale jogged ahead a few steps in order to accommodate the generals' quick, angry pace.

As they neared the machine gun Gale called out to announce their presence. "Sergeant Sheppard, General Haig and General Foch are here!"

The entire team immediately leaped off the trench wall and stood at attention. Sergeant Sheppard, Charles, and Thomas all stood at attention and saluted. "I have heard a lot of rumors, Sergeant Sheppard," Haig began, "of some nearly traitorous activities that happened here on Christmas Eve and Christmas Day. Do you know what I am speaking about?"

"I don't believe so, sir," Sheppard said.

"Then let me enlighten you. I received a dispatch that your team, along with countless others in the trench all crossed into No Man's land and fraternized with the enemy. Some reports say your team even played a game of football with them. Is that true?"

"It is, sir."

"Do you know what is wrong with that?"

"No, sir. I had believed that the truce had been sanctioned, sir."

"It wasn't. You and your team made a mockery of the British and French armies. News of this ... unauthorized truce, of the ... soiree you had with German soldiers has made it back to England. It has made us look like we decided to waste important rations meant to boost our own troops morale over the holiday on the enemy. You and your team have spat in the face of the British and French people. Because of that, your team, along with others, will have to be punished. You will be on quarter rations for a month, understand?"

"I—yes, sir," Sheppard said. Gale watched the interaction, he could barely believe what he was hearing. Quarter rations? For a month. In midwinter? The watered-down soup was barely enough to sustain them, now in addition to being cold and damp all the time, they were also going to be hungry? And for what? Having a moment of civility on the battlefield?

"Also, while I am here," Haig said, "I will be sending part of your team on a campaign to Gallipoli. They've all shown themselves to be more than capable and would be great assets. I'd like you to choose now," Haig continued, he had a gleam in his eye that made Gale's hair on the back of his neck stand on end. It was the kind of look that said he knew he was being unfair and cruel in his demand but didn't care, reveled in it even. By the way Sheppard's back straightened more and more with every word Haig said, he too was on edge.

"Now, sir?" Sheppard asked.

"Yes, Sergeant, do you have a problem with that?" Haig leaned forward, and while Sheppard was taller than him, he was broader and gave off a menacing air.

"No, sir," Sheppard started. He looked between the team, his eyes had a sad look to them, his lips formed a tight line, the creases of frustration that Gale had observed when he had first encountered Sheppard had completely returned. "Privates Dunford, Abbey, and Rory McGuinness are fine soldiers and will serve with valor," he said, after a beat.

Charles was going, and he wasn't? Gale had always known it was likely for their team to be split up. That one day they'd get assignments that would take them to different theaters of war. Gale had just always assumed that he and Charles would stick together. He was his brother in all ways but blood. Although, if Gale thought back, he might remember his seven-year-old self taking a needle to prick his and Charles' fingertips to mix their blood as they swore an oath to be brothers. But, at the moment, Gale was far too caught up in the idea that he was going to be split off from his best friend. That Charles was going to be almost an entire continent away in Gallipoli.

"Very good. They'll get orders shortly and will ship out in seven days," General Haig said. "Now, excuse us, we have a lot of teams to get through." Without another word Haig, Foch, and their posse of lieutenants were off. It struck Gale how little they really seemed to care about the effects of their words on the soldiers under them. It reminded Gale of Charles' father. Upper class, unbothered by the idea that his words and actions impact others beyond bidding them to do what he wanted. Maybe that was the reason he felt on edge. He looked to Charles who had an expression on his face that said he had also made the connection between Haig and his father. Gale shared a look with Charles to let him know that he saw the connection too and that it wasn't unnoticed.

Silence fell over the team allowing the voices of Haig and Foch chastising another team of soldiers in the regiment. "Are they really spending their day personally punishing all of us?" Rory asked, disbelief in his tone.

"Seems like it," Thomas replied.

"Right, good to know they're thinking about the best strategies to win the war with," Rory replied bitterly.

Instead of the usual warning that Rory would get for such a comment, Sheppard just hummed in agreement. "Okay, lads, back to our stations. Gale, Barry, Arthur, Finn, get some rest."

Gale wanted to protest, he wanted to check in with his brother. He was shipping out in a week. It was then that Gale realized that this must have been what his family felt like when he announced they would be leaving soon. On one hand, there was a sense of pride that Charles got picked to go. Gale knew he was going to do well; he'd keep the others safe. On the other, Gale wished he could be there to make sure someone was watching Charles' back. He knew it was going to be strange no matter what, after all, the two hadn't spent more than a few weeks apart at a time since childhood.

A week passed quickly as a somber mood had fallen over the Sheppard team. All of them knew that they were going to be split. They had grown close as true brothers in arms. The night before Charles, Rory, and Thomas were to ship out, Sheppard broke out what was left of the whiskey from Christmas.

"It seems fitting that we started the bottle together, and we should end it together as well," Sheppard said. The group stayed up late, huddled around a fire, playing cards and drinking until dawn slowly started to creep up the horizon. They started to say their goodbyes, knowing it would only be a matter of minutes until the Gallipoli-bound boys had the leave. Gale said his goodbye to Thomas and Rory. He was going to miss those two. The sense of calm that Thomas brought to the group and the brash chaos that seemed to follow Rory everywhere he went. Then, it was time to say goodbye to Charles.

"You're not allowed to die," Gale said sternly as he gave Charles a quick hug. "Not only would your father skin me alive, but so would my own."

"Funny, I was about to say the same thing," Charles replied. "Right, well, we better be off, then. I'll see you when we've tamed the Ottomans," he said, taking a step back from Gale.

"Or when we've beaten the Huns back to their home," Gale said.

The Gallipoli group started to head off, making their way to the transport, when Gale could swear he heard Rory say, "Wait, I thought Gallipoli was in Italy, not in the heart of the Ottoman." Gale couldn't help but laugh.

CHAPTER 10

March 10th, 1915

The morning of March tenth was a mess. It was foggy and raining. The trampled earth in the trenches had turned into a massive mud pit. Gale could feel his feet sinking with each step. It wasn't quite dawn yet, but Gale and the rest of Sheppard's team were mobilizing and were joining a detachment near Neuve Chapelle. They had to head out so early because they couldn't alert the Germans to the British Armies movements. Sheppard had grumbled a bit when they had gotten their assignments, they found out they were going to be following one of the Indian troop brigades. Which one Gale couldn't quite remember because Sheppard had been far too annoyed to repeat the name after he spat it out.

The team moved in silence through the trench, deftly passing other teams getting ready for the assault. Some were staying in their place to draw attention from the intended target of the assault: the communication lines. By severing them, it seemed that the strategy was intended to confuse the German army long enough for the British and French to secure more territory in the Artois region. Gale was cautiously optimistic about this plan. It seemed like the first time in a long time that there was a clear strategy for a battle. They had a goal to work toward, and that was when Gale shined; he knew that for a fact.

It gave him something to go for instead of just trying to stay afloat during what felt like an unending onslaught of enemy combatants. Sheppard seemed to have similar feelings about that part of the operation—it was clear that was the only part that Sheppard was happy about.

"You can't trust them," Sheppard had said.

"Who? The Indians?" Gale asked.

"Yes, the Indians, who else?"

"Isn't your wife Indian?" Finn asked. It was a good question, one that Gale was wondering too.

"That's different," Sheppard said after a beat. He marched out of the dugout after that to take a smoke break.

"That was ... odd," Arthur said.

"Yeah, makes me wonder where that came from," Barry said, "I didn't realize he felt that way, especially since his wife—"

Instead of listening to them guess at what the issue was, Gale got up. "I'm just going to ask him. We're his team, we should know. If he's got a good reason, we should know. After all, he was posted in India." Before the others had a chance to stop him, Gale headed out to find their sergeant. He didn't have to look for too long, Sheppard was leaning against the trench wall near the machine gun station.

"Sir," Gale started.

Sheppard held up his hand. "Arlington, not now."

"But—"

"I mean it, don't make me turn it into an order."

"Sir, if you think they aren't trustworthy then we should know why, we're about to go into battle with them."

"It's personal."

"Even so, I trust your instincts sir, if you aren't sure about this, we should know so we can be on guard," Gale pushed.

"It has nothing to do with ... they're on our side, you can trust them with the mission. They might not have your back, but they won't stab it while you're not looking. Don't worry about it." Sheppard's tone was final, but it sounded like there was much more to be said. Gale shifted his weight, he wasn't sure what else he could say. "Arlington, there's nothing else to say. Get some rest; we head out early."

Gale rolled his eyes but headed back to the dugout. He wondered if Sheppard realized that he was essentially making him go to his room because he simply didn't want to answer any of Gale's questions.

As the team finally met up with the Indian troops after navigating miles of trenches, it was only minutes before the assault was meant to begin at 7:30 in the morning. Gale loaded his gun and made sure his bayonet was tightly fixed to the end of his rifle. They are still in the trench and it was almost time for it to begin. Gale took a deep breath. He looked at Finn, Barry, and Arthur. They all looked as serious and determined as he felt. The Indian soldiers barely paid them any attention and it seemed that Sheppard was happy with it. There was a man at the front who looked more ready to climb the trenches and fight than any of them there. He didn't understand Urdu, but it seemed like the other Indian soldiers kept calling him Jagali, and they spoke with a certain amount of reverence that surprised Gale. He wondered if Jagali was the brigade commander or if he just had great fighting prowess.

They were waiting for the artillery to start the assault. When they had arrived at the rendezvous location in the Indian troops' section of trenches, Gale had seen the massive 18-pounder guns ready to shoot. It was going to be loud and, with any luck, it would do enough to sever German communications. Gale knew that as the artillery began their assault, the Royal Flying Corps would start theirs, bombing the ground and shooting the supply lines. Gale really hoped this mission was as carefully coordinated as it sounded like it was meant to be.

The final minute before the operation began was slower than molasses pouring from a bottle on a cold winter day. Gale wanted nothing more than for it to start. His heart was racing, his pulse thumping loudly in his ears. He took a deep breath and got ready to take the position of the Indian soldier in front of him. It was their job to cover the Indian brigade as they forced their way forward through

No Man's land. Even with the artillery cover and the RFC's attacks, it was still a risky position to be in. Despite Sheppard's concern about the Indian soldiers not caring about watching their backs, Gale was going to do all he could in his power to protect the men in front of him.

With a loud bang, the first cannon shot off, announcing the start of their side's attack on the German army. It was followed by dozens more artillery guns shooting. The Indian brigade took off over the trench wall. Gale, Arthur, Barry, Finn, and Sheppard quickly climbed up the trench wall and took the position of the soldiers in front of them. They gunned down as many German soldiers as they could, keeping the threats away from the line of Indian soldiers moving through the wasteland. It was clear even from far across the way, the German soldier's were scrambling. The Indian brigades were going to make it through the German line and push through. Even though the battle had just begun, it was clear that the British Empire was going to succeed in the plan, of which Gale was sure.

Sheppard's team held their position, keeping back any German soldiers that somehow managed to get past the Indian line. Finally, Sheppard received the order to advance his team into the fray. They were to hold the flank as the Germans tried to push back. Sheppard immediately set off into No Man's land, following the Indian line. Gale and the rest of the team were quick to follow behind. It was the first time that Gale had been in No Man's land since the fateful Christmas truce and the first time he'd ever been in it while being shot at. Artillery shells were arcing through the sky above them from both sides. By Gale's estimation theirs were bigger, causing more shrapnel and explosive damage. They fought for hours through No Man's land until they reached the trench. Gale and the rest of the team focused their attention on taking the trench. They quickly flushed any of the remaining German soldiers out of their dugouts. None surrendered to be taken prisoner, instead they elected to fight or run. Most were smart enough to run. There would be no reinforcements coming for them. Loud roars of plane engines flying near their targets managed to cut the sound of artillery fire.

Gale and the others moved with synchronized precision and made quick work of capturing the trench. "We're going to hold our position here and wait for orders," Sheppard said. It was a fairly easy task to maintain their control of the trench. There was no soldier contesting it. The beginning of the operation was going successfully. Finally, some of the Indian brigade returned, joining Sheppard's team in the trench. A man walked up the Sheppard, from his uniform, he must have been a fellow sergeant.

"We are to stay here until the morning. And then we're to press on," he said.

"That so?" Sheppard asked, "Do you have the orders in writing?"

The other sergeant didn't react to the hostile tone in Sheppard's voice, even if his eye seemed to twitch out of annoyance just a touch. He reached into his jacket pocket and pulled out a telegram and handed it to Sheppard to read. Sheppard took it and looked the telegram over. He nodded, seemingly satisfied and handed it back.

"Very good," Sheppard said. "We'll take these dugouts," he added, pointing to some a little further afield from the dugout where some of the Indian soldiers were making themselves comfortable.

"Very well, if that's what you'd like," the other sergeant said. Before they could head their separate ways the intense man from before climbed back over the trench wall into No Man's land. Sheppard's team watched him as he surveyed the ground. He stopped in front of a German soldier's corpse and grabbed his head. Then, in two quick movements, he cut the soldier's eyes out. Gale could feel the blood drain from his face as he watched the man toss the soldier's body back down. He repeated the action. Over and over again. The Indian sergeant followed their gaze, he seemed unaffected by what his fellow soldier was doing. He then turned back to Sheppard and his team.

"That is Jagali, he's our leader, one of the best soldiers in the empire. He has the highest kill count," the sergeant replied easily, as if he were simply stating the type of weather to expect for the next day.

Gale and the rest of the team could barely take their eyes away from what Jagali was doing to fully acknowledge what the Indian sergeant had just told them. Then, as if he knew they were watching, Jagali turned and made direct eye contact with Sheppard. The two held a steely gaze. Then, before anyone could say anything, Jagali returned to his strange and sickening ritual.

"Right," Sheppard said, after a beat, "let's get stuck in and start to plan our next move."

CHAPTER 11

March 11th, 1915

Sheppard's team had spent the rest of the day and night going over the small map they had of the area surrounding the French town they were reclaiming, Neuve Chappelle. "Our main goal tomorrow is to take the garrison just beyond this trench. The Germans are already on the run, as long as they aren't able to regroup tonight. Luckily the artillery and the RFC is on that," Sheppard said, explaining what they would be doing in the morning.

"Just fighting straight through, then," Arthur said.

"Yes, sounds simple enough, and we're good enough to make quick work of it, right, boys?"

"Yes, sir!" Barry, Gale, and Arthur said in unison. Sheppard gave them a smile that made it clear that they were. That night, Gale lay awake. He had gotten used to the feeling by now, the nerves mingled with excitement. The way that exhaustion pulled at him but wasn't quite strong enough to overcome the other feelings. He knew that eventually, he would be able to manage to get an hour or two and then once they had gotten through the fight and secured the garrison, he'd be able to sleep like a dream. Gale never used to be that driven by the idea of when he would be able to sleep next, but the longer he spent on the front the more he found himself longing for a good night's rest. Or a day or two to really relax. Or even a warm bath. Really, anything that seemed remotely like a creature comforts. Gale knew that fantasizing about a soft bed and full belly wasn't going to do him any good. The longer he lingered on those thoughts, the longer it took him to adjust to the reality of the situation. War was hard, it was a crucible, and he knew that he was going to emerge a better man.

He thought about the stories the way his grandad had talked about war. He had always been honest about the difficulties that he faced during the Crimean War. The pain and grief he had felt, the horrors he had seen in the cavalry. Gale couldn't help but wonder what his grandad would think about the way the cavalry was getting mowed down by the machine guns? Despite the honesty and bluntness that Gale's grandad had used while telling his war stories, he also talked about how it made him into the man he was. His father had said the same to Gale growing up. So, now, as Gale laid in the dugout of the trench he had taken from the German's that night, he comforted himself with the idea that the discomfort and stress he was feeling would turn him into the men that his father and grandfather were.

Finally, Gale managed to fall asleep. He didn't dream that night, rather, he let the darkness of unconsciousness take over him. Then, in what felt like minutes, but was in reality a couple hours, Gale was startled awake with the rest of the team. The sound of artillery fire, plane engines, and high-pitched whistles seemed to come out of nowhere, shattering the peaceful quiet of the early morning. The team was quick to get up and recover their bearings. Gale grabbed his rifle and loaded a magazine of bullets, pulling the bolt to ensure there was a charge in the chamber ready to go.

Sheppard looked over his men and nodded that he was satisfied with them. "Alright, men, let's move out." The team charged out of the dugout and sprinted up the side of the trench. They kept their pace up as they ran the distance over the field toward the battle that had broken out. It was clear that while they had slept at night, Sheppard's worst fears had been confirmed; the Germans had had enough time to regroup and gather some reinforcements.

"Where did they come from?" Barry yelled over the noise.

"They're all the ones that survived the first attack!" Arthur yelled. The group managed to reach the fray unscathed, just in time for them to start attacking a group of German soldiers that had made it past the Indian forces. Gale shot one running toward him and then switched to using his bayonet. He managed to fell another German soldier, then, out of the corner of his eye, he saw Finn was getting overwhelmed by another group of Germans. Gale slashed his way through the soldiers standing in his way, and he forged a path to help out Finn. Together the two managed to injure or kill the group that had surrounded Finn. Gale realized that he hadn't really ever fought beside Finn. The two of them were agile and dexterous. They were able to easily outmaneuver most soldiers coming their way.

It wasn't until Gale and Finn had defended themselves against the last of the German soldiers that had been part of the onslaught against Finn, that the two realized they had been separated from the rest of their team. "Which way did they go?" Finn asked. "Should we start to look for them?" Gale looked around the battlefield. He had no clue where the others had gone. He couldn't even pick out Arthur's large form from the other soldiers.

"They must be all on the other side," Gale concluded. Then, he looked forward and saw a large limestone building. It was surrounded by abandoned artillery guns. Much of it had already started to crumble from all of the explosive shells aimed at it by the British armies. "That's the garrison," he realized. "That's where we have to go. We'll find our team there. C'mon Finn!" Gale grabbed Finn's arm and the two of them sprinted to the garrison. It wasn't hard for them to find an entrance since one of the walls was all but fallen. It was oddly quiet when they stepped into the building.

"It's like a mausoleum," Finn commented.

Gale nodded, it was eerie, and he didn't trust it. He was about to tell Finn to stay on guard when he heard a pebble get kicked out from around a corner. It skittered across the marble floor, echoing in the empty space. Gale held out his arm, stopping Finn. He nodded in the direction of the corner as if to warn Finn that someone was back there, waiting for them. Gale lifted up his rifle, and counted the number of bullets he had left in his magazine. Three. Finn did the same. With their rifles at the ready, the two of them slowly crept forward. Then, before they could get a look at who was behind the corner waiting for them, a group of German infantry jumped out and ambushed them. Gale and Finn shot into the mob. They both managed to hit a soldier each, but it wasn't enough they shot again and again. Gale was out of bullets. Finn was able to get one more shot in. Their attacks only seemed to enrage the German soldiers, they started to attack back, waving their bayonets, trying to cut or stab either of them.

It was then that Gale realized they were out of ammunition too. They just had to outrun them long enough to find the rest of their team. Or really any friendly soldier. British, French, Indian, even Canadian. As Gale watched the Germans approach in a line. Each soldier was evenly spaced out. He remembered when he was a kid playing the game Red Rover. He always would look for those sorts of gaps to break through the line. "Do you trust me?" Gale asked as they backed up further from the mob of German infantrymen.

"With languages? No. But with this, yes, implicitly," Finn said. Gale laughed—his friend still sounded like he always did, even when they were being backed into the wall. Gale brandished his rifle like it was a sword ready to fight back against any of the soldiers in their way. "Ready?" he whispered.

Instead of speaking, Finn gave a small, just barely perceivable nod. Gale grabbed his arm and the two started to run, charging at the Germans. The enemy soldiers were shocked at their brazen approach. Gale and Finn forced their way through the lines of Germans and sprinted away down the corridor. The Germans turned and started to pursue them. The two of them turned a corner and ran directly into Jagali.

"Who are you—"

"Germans were hiding, we found them," Gale explained, out of breath.

"Technically they found us," Finn argued. Jagali and the men behind them lifted their rifles just in time for them to hear the thundering footsteps of Gale and Finn's German pursuers. Jagali and his men stepped around the corner into the hallway where the Germans were. Before Gale realized exactly what was happening, he heard the sound of guns firing. Then the heavy sound of bodies falling back and hitting the floor. Jagali and the riflemen behind him quickly returned. It was clear what had happened, and they seemed beyond unbothered.

"Come with me," Jagali said as he and his men walked past Finn and Gale. Jagali didn't spare another look at either of them as he reloaded his rifle and lifted it up. Gale and Finn looked at each other. The Indian soldier was their best bet to get back to their team, both of them knew it. Gale made quick work of reloading his gun with new bullets and pulling the bolt. He followed Jagali's lead and lifted the rifle up so he would be ready to shoot if there was another ambush. The five of them continued to move through the hallways of the garrison building. From the outside, the limestone building hadn't seemed like it was too large. But as the group painstakingly cleared corridor after corridor and room after room, Gale realized his estimation was sorely incorrect.

"Strange how this building has a combination of Gothic and Neoclassical architecture," Finn whispered to Gale.

Gale turned to Finn and saw that his friend was looking at the conical ceilings being held up by smooth white marble pillars. Gale wanted to ask why Finn even noticed the architecture at a time like this.

"They must have rebuilt it," Finn elaborated. "That's why the corridors feel so endless," he added.

Jagali turned around and looked at Finn. "Explain," he said.

"Well, the renovation obviously tried to make it ...this building, that is, fit with the Neoclassical ideals that the French government is founded on, you see, that was the style that was popular in 1789 during the French Revolution. It was the Neo-classics who brought back Greek philosophy and the belief of secularism—"

"I meant that you needed to explain about the corridors, this building. I didn't ask for a history lesson," Jagali said impatiently.

"Oh, well it's not that big of a deal; it's just that some of the corridors feed into each other. They added on so some of them are redun-dant. Like the one Gale and I were running down when we met up with you ..." Finn said, trailing off as Jagali's stare grew even more intense.

"Do you think there are hallways we've missed?" he asked.

"I don't think so, I just think that we should all be aware of them."

Jagali nodded, satisfied with Finn's answer. "Good, thank you for pointing that out." Gale was reminded a bit of Sheppard, their movements and mannerisms were similar.

The band of five continued onward through the building until Jagali was convinced that they had indeed gone through every inch of the garrison. "It's clear, we have taken the garrison," he said with a small smile.

Gale couldn't help himself; he let out a whoop of excitement and Finn joined him. Jagali raised his eyebrows at them. The two other riflemen carried very similar expressions to their captain.

"Do you do that after every victory?" Jagali asked.

"Only the exciting ones," Gale laughed.

Jagali sighed. Gale wasn't sure if the look on the Captain's face was more amused or exasperated. Gale decided it was a combination of both. He felt happy-go-lucky and nothing was going to bring him down from it, Gale decided. He had escaped many near-death experiences within one battle. "Don't be too excited—just because we have broken through doesn't mean the battle is won."

"Yes, sir," Gale said. The happy-go-lucky feeling was quickly deflated by Jagali's comment.

"Let's go get you back to your sergeant. Don't want him to think that we've sent you into the enemy's clutches," Jagali said. Gale and Finn shared a look. How could Jagali possibly know about the exact distrust that Sheppard had for the Indian troops? Did he say it to their faces? He had been abrupt and didn't exactly do anything to hide his dislike of them. But, surely he hadn't said that he thought they wouldn't be afraid to leave their fellow soldier out to dry.

Before Gale or Finn could protest that comment, Jagali headed off

CHAPTER 12

March 12th, 1915

Gale waited quietly, absentmindedly kicking at the dirt as Sheppard finished reading the missive sent to them by command. There was an electricity in the air that came only from the success of missions and battle plans. Gale hadn't realized how much he desperately missed the lighter feeling that came along with winning. The feeling that there was light at the end of the battle and not just a tactical retreat. They weren't just holding the line they were going to advance it, he felt it in his bones. The tightness that had settled in his chest—making his breath feel pinched and cut off—seemed to release just enough that he wasn't on edge every second of the day.

"Alright men, we are going to move forward. Just beyond the garrison there is another line of trenches between us and the Hun headquarters. It's our job to storm the trench and hold it with our Indian counterparts. Got it?" Sheppard looked at each member of his team one at a time, starting with Arthur, then Gale, Finn, and finally Barry.

"Yes, sir!" they all replied in quick unison. Gale barely even registered saying that phrase anymore. He said it almost as often as he breathed it had become that much of a second nature to him. It was the same with how he stood at attention, his back straightened and shoulders back. *It was almost more comfortable to stand like that then slouched ... almost*, he thought. Even with all of the excitement that came from finally having the advantage on the battlefield after what felt like months of barely holding their ground, his exhaustion did tug at the back of his mind. His muscles were always trying to pull him downward in tandem with the natural laws of gravity that made the drag to the ground all the more enticing. Gale shook his head, clearing his mind of that thought. Now was not the time to think about rest. Now was the time to think about the opportunity they were going to seize for the Allied armies. He wondered now if Foch and Haig regretted putting him and his team on quarter rations, after all the amount of progress they had gotten almost single-handedly, surely was enough to forgive the whole Christmas thing. They probably didn't spare a second thought to the matter, realistically, however, Gale couldn't help but want to believe they did.

"Right men, on my orders we'll move out," Sheppard said. Gale and the rest of the team waited with bated breaths for the sergeant's signal. Each of them loaded their guns and made sure their bayonets were tightly secured. The more they fought, the more often they had to fight using a combination of long distance and close-range combat. Gale had learned how to clean his bayonet until it looked like there hadn't been a single droplet of blood to touch it. Gale had to admit that he had grown a little fanatical about it in the past few months, but it bothered him, perhaps more than others, to have a dead man's blood soaking into the steel.

As Gale waited for Sheppard's signal, he wondered if there was a specific time given for them to move out, or if they were to wait for the cavalry to ride by, breaking through the beginning of the reestablished German lines. Gale wondered if the Germans had managed to recuperate or if they would still be licking their wounds. Gale turned his head looking down the line. It was always interesting to him how each team member settled themselves as they waited. Arthur always leaned forward like he was about to compete in a race, his feet dug into the ground, his shoulders far back. Finn stood straight, like he didn't move at all. Rather, he looked like he was in the process of turning into a stone statue, his face was blank, almost as if his soul and mind had completely left his body. Barry was the opposite, he was twitchy, constantly shifting from foot to foot, antsy to move. He checked and rechecked his rifle and bayonet, like he couldn't trust his memory to ensure that he had indeed already loaded it and secured the blade.

They didn't have to wait too long for the order to move. It turned out it wasn't by time or by cavalry moving out. But rather, by artillery fire, just like the day before. The loud explosions and pattering sounds of dirt falling in a spray back to the ground should be just as common-place as the sound of cocking and firing a rifle. But the initial wave of fire from the massive guns at the rear of the line always rattle Gale to his core. His ears rung in tandem to the vibrations sent through the earth by each impact of exploding shell and cannonball.

"Let's go!" Sheppard yelled, the booming of his voice barely loud enough to be heard over the fire. The team sprinted, a large stretch of abandoned German territory ahead of them. They passed the garrison that Gale and Finn had helped to clear. As they passed it, Gale saw the tell-tale signs of a battle that had long since ended, at first he was confused, but as he ran toward the outskirts of the small French town, Gale realized that this was the site of a battle where Germany had first invaded France, long before Gale or any of the rest of the team had reached the battlefield. He didn't let himself wonder what would have happened if the French were able to stop the German invasion, or if the British had come the second it seemed like Germany was going to take advantage of the archduke's assassination and use it as an excuse to press forward. Thinking about that as he was aiming his rifle at a German soldier was the last thing he needed. As he exhaled, he forced those thoughts out of his mind then pulled the trigger. It was a direct hit. The soldier stumbled backward and fell to the ground. That was when the real fighting began.

Gale and the rest of the team fought their way through the fray until finally they were getting within sight of the trench they were meant to take. But as they got closer, a band of German soldiers climbed up and over the trench parapet. Artillery and machine guns were firing from both sides, cutting soldiers down left and right. Gale took aim at one of the German soldiers and fired. He grazed the man's shoulder, and Gale grimaced. At this point he had gotten used to better accuracy with his shot. However, instead of letting it distract him, he continued to shoot, doing his best to bring down as many enemy soldiers as he could. Getting into close-range combat would be dangerous. Especially since these soldiers seemed much better rested and ready to fight than the ones from the night before. Keeping them further away than arm's length was the best bet. Gale looked at the rest of the team; they all had the same determined look in their eyes that said they had the same idea too.

They were making slow progress to the trench, they had to work slowly, every centimeter was hard won and easily lost. It felt as though they were playing a deadly game of tug-o-war over a mere few meters. Every time it felt like they were making any progress, they were pushed back just as far. They were being met blow for blow. It was getting too dangerous to stay there.

"Boys, we need cover or we're going to lose some of our own!" Sheppard yelled just as he started to squeeze the trigger of his rifle. Gale immediately pulled back a bit behind the staggered line that the team had formed and looked for a place they could hunker down behind. They were once again in a field, so the land was flat and didn't have much in terms of natural barriers, aside from the mortar holes that now peppered the landscape. Those could serve to hide one or two of them, but an entire team would face certain death. But, over a dozen or so meters to the northwest of their location was a turned-over truck. Memories of the first day of fighting, of Michael being shot and hitting the ground from behind an almost identical vehicle flooded Gale. But they didn't have time to look for a second option. "Sergeant, over there!" Gale yelled, pointing to the truck.

The sergeant, keeping his eyes firmly on a German soldier in the distance, tilted his head in the direction of where Gale was pointing. "Men!" he yelled, "to the truck! Keep your rifles locked and loaded!" The team began to make the run to their new cover. Each of them kept most of their focus on shooting at the enemy infantrymen, keeping their aim at them as the team ran. A barrage of bullets rained down around them, again Gale thanked God that he wasn't hit. He turned and aimed toward the machine gun, trying to hit the soldier feeding the magazines into the gun. Finn stopped with him. Between the two of them, they were able to take out the machine gun, at least temporarily.

Just as Gale and Finn were about to turn around and make a run for the last couple of meters to cover, Gale heard the beginning of another wave of gunfire. He turned just in time to see Finn stumble backward, crying out in pain. He clutched at his side. Gale ran up to him, grabbing him before he fell to get ground. Gale wrapped one of Finn's arms over his shoulder and wrapped his own arm around Finn's waist, careful to avoid the bullet wound. Finn hissed in pain. "Gale, you need to go!"

"No, I promised to have your back. We're going to make it to cover together." How, Gale wasn't so sure. But he wasn't going to tell Finn that. He needed to come up with a plan. He looked at the truck where the rest of the team had made it too, safely. With the amount of fire they were dealing with and with no way for Gale or Finn to be able to use their rifles to defend themselves, the meters of distance they had left to cross might as well have been miles. "Okay, we need to find a cover until the fighting stops, okay ... okay, Finn?"

Finn swallowed hard. His breathing was ragged, face sweating and twisted in pain. "Okay," Finn agreed, speaking through his clenched teeth.

"Good," Gale said, relieved that Finn was able to speak, even if it was hard. It meant that he was able to breath, so his lungs weren't damaged, and his speech wasn't gargled with blood, so there was a very low chance the bullet had hit anything too important. Gale really hoped that it had just hit fat and muscle tissue of the torso, avoiding any of the organs. He needed Finn to make it. Just when Gale was about to give up on finding a nearby spot to hunker down and attempt the no doubt deadly trek to truck for cover, he spotted a mortar hole just a meter or two over. "C'mon, I found a place, think you can make it there?" Gale asked, pointing to the hole.

Finn nodded, "Yeah, I think so." His breathing was still rough, so Gale knew he had to get him off his feet and check out his injury sooner than later.

Gale held Finn tightly and shifted his friend so he was supporting the bulk of his weight. Gale made sure to hunch over, trying to minimize his and Finn's bodies as much as possible. He didn't want to make them even more vulnerable to gunfire. They were big enough targets as it were. They made it to the mortar hole and crawled in. Gale was relieved to discover that it was indeed deep enough for him to tuck Finn and himself below the upper rim of it. Before Gale let himself relax, he made sure to tighten the leather strap that held Finn's helmet on his head. The last thing that he wanted to worry about was the helmet slipping out of the way and a freak shot getting his friend killed. He refused to let that happen. Without letting himself catch his breath, Gale pulled out his field kit. "Dammit," he said. He was low on supplies, but there seemed to be just enough bandages to at least secure what little gauze he had. He grabbed the small bottle of iodine and held it up to the little light that was coming from the setting sun. The sun's orange rays shined through the brown glass of the bottle, revealing what Gale had suspected. There was barely any left in the bottom. Then, he remembered that Finn had always made a point of collecting as many first-aid supplies as possible. Without wasting a beat, Gale began to search through Finn's webbing to find the pouch that he kept it all in.

"What are you ...?" Finn started to ask.

"Medkit?" Gale replied.

"Top right," Finn managed to get out.

Gale quickly reached into the top right pocket of Finn's vest and pulled out a small brass tin. He opened it and found a neatly packed med kit. There was gauze, bandages, a needle, thread, and most importantly, a full bottle of iodine. He knew he had to get as much into Finn's wound as possible before an infection had a chance to set in. And on the battlefield, Gale was all too aware of how little time it took for germs to get into wounds and wreak havoc. More soldiers had been sent behind the lines with the nurses because of infection than injury, or at least from what he could tell. Gale wasted no time pulling away Finn's vest, jacket, and shirt out of the way. The wound wasn't deep, it had been slowed by the thick wool of the British uniform, and the tightly woven canvas straps that made up the webbing of their vests. The bullet looked like it had barely been able to lodge itself into the flesh about Finn's hip bone. Gale was no doctor, but to him it didn't look too bad. Or rather, not as bad as it could have looked. Blood coated Finn's skin with a sticky slick. The skin was red and angry, the hole formed by the bullet was ragged and uneven. He wondered how a surgeon could even take the tattered skin and close the wound with it. Or worse, if he would be able to.

"Should I take it out?" He asked, he sounded as helpless as he felt.

"No!" Finn said, quickly. "Don't. It's like a stab wound. Just ... cover it with iodine and bandage it."

Like a stab wound? Gale had no idea what Finn meant by that, but he trusted his friend to know better than he did. Gale dumped out what was left in his iodine bottle and then did the same with Finn. The brown solution mixed with the blood that was oozing from the wound, making a rusty liquid that covered Finn's pale freckled skin.

It gave Gale a sense of relief when the angry red of the flesh surrounding the bullet wound was masked by the iodine. Then they packed the wound with gauze and began to wrap bandages around Finn's waist. It was awkward and slow going, as he had to lift Finn up just enough that he could get the roll of bandages all the way around his body. But, finally Gale was satisfied with his handy work.

"How are you feeling?" Gale asked.

"Perfectly delightful," Finn mumbled. "Never been better, thanks."

"You can't fall asleep yet," Gale said.

Finn groaned, "Fine." Gale had to laugh; he sounded like a petulant child.

"I mean it. I need to make sure that you're not bleeding," Gale said, doing his best impression of Gale Sr.'s stern voice reserved only for when he was telling Gale off after he did something daft.

"I'm fairly certain that I'm going to keep bleeding until I get stitched up, alright?" Finn replied. It was moments like this, when Finn was tired or drunk or stressed, that he sounded more like his brothers. He usually did his best to sound as formal as possible as often as possible. The sass of his response made it clear that Gale's attempt at being stern wasn't working. Clearly, he had not mastered the tone.

Gunfire continued to rain down and artillery shells shot through the sky. The two boys huddled down, pressing tightly to the edge of the mortar hole to do their best to stay as camouflaged as possible. "We're stuck here, aren't we?" Finn said in between blasts.

"Looks like it, best get comfortable, mate," Gale said.

"You should have just left me here," Finn half whispered.

"Finn, you're my friend, my brother in arms. I'm not going to just leave you. Besides, we help each other, that's what we do," Gale replied. Finn scoffed, then groaned. "I'm serious, Finn. We promised each other before we were shipped out. We stand by each other. That's it. That simple."

"I bet Sarge is having kittens over this."

"You kidding, he's probably about ready to chew glass," Gale laughed. "'Specially since we'd already separated from the team just yesterday."

"We've got to stop doing that," Finn laughed. He shifted up and then winced.

"Don't sit up, the wound is right above your hip."

"Yup, I was able to discern that much," Finn said dryly.

"I'm just saying," Gale replied, surrendering. It wasn't worth getting into it with Finn over his own bullet wound. The two boys waited, cringing as the ground shook from explosions as shells buried themselves into the earth. The longer they sat there, the longer the more dirt they were getting covered in. On one hand it helped to keep them hidden from German soldiers, on the other, Gale couldn't help but worry about the chance of infection. "Well, think of it this way, when you get back home, you'll have a great battle story to woo the birds with."

"Ha, sure," Finn said, "if I get back."

"Nope, you don't get to say that. You're going to be fine. Some of the best doctors in the nation are with the army. We'll get you patched up, good as new, before you can even say Bob's your uncle," Gale answered quickly. He wasn't going to let his friend get fatalistic. "You're going to be fine," he added.

"Okay, okay, I believe you," Finn replied, he sounded more resigned than convinced, but Gale was going to take that as a win. The two waited and waited, the sun lowered further and further below the horizon. The sky darkened, and they were left with light that came from the sliver of pale moonlight and the flashes of gunfire that was still traded between the two trenches. Gale's stomach growled. The adrenaline was wearing off, and he was slowly becoming aware of his bodily needs. His mouth was dry, and he could feel a tickle at the back of his throat that wasn't going to go away anytime soon. He grabbed his canteen and found it empty.

"I'm out too," Finn said, before Gale could ask. "Believe me, I've already checked."

Gale nodded and cleared his throat. It did little to stave off the cotton ball mouth feeling he had, but he no longer felt like he was seconds away from hacking out a lung or two. Then Gale realized he couldn't hear any gunfire.

"Do we move?" Gale whispered, reluctant to break the silence of the night's stalemate.

"I want to but ..."

"It might restart the fire fight if we get seen," Gale said, finishing Finn's sentence. They both knew what happened to people caught in No Man's land. Both sides had a pretty strict policy to shoot anything that moves at night.

"Arlington, McGuinness!" Finn and Gale immediately perk up, it was the sergeant yelling.

"Sarge?" Gale yelled back.

"Report!"

Gale wanted to roll his eyes, was he supposed to yell their location to anyone out there? "We're fine, just stuck!" He hoped that the sergeant would be satisfied with that.

There was a beat and then the sarge yelled again. "Stay put! Await instructions!"

"Yessir!" Finn and Gale yelled in unison. It felt foolish for them to be yelling at each other. What if a German soldier decided to cut the conversation short for them? Gale turned to Finn and could just make out the same confused expression on his friend's face that was no doubt on his in the moonlight.

"How are we even supposed to get instructions?" Finn griped. "He's all the way over there," he added, gesturing in the direction of the truck.

"I'm sure he's got something figured out," Gale said. He just hoped that was true. Then, before either boy could say anything else of substance, they heard the breaking of a branch coming their way. It sounded like it was coming from the direction of Allied armies. Regardless, Gale lifted his rifle and pointed it in the direction of the noise.

"Put that thing down. You're going to take someone's eye out," a very familiar voice whispered. It was Arthur. Gale immediately put the rifle down as Arthur crawled his way into the mortar hole with them. Gale and Finn shifted to accommodate Arthur. He made his way so he was sitting shoulder to shoulder and with Finn. "You alright? I saw you go down?"

"Just a small bullet wound," Finn said, "Gale's set me right, for now."

"Oh, if that's all," Arthur said, annoyed.

"That it is," Finn retorted. "What in God's good name are you doing out here?"

"I was wondering the same," Gale added.

Arthur shifted and pulled out a couple packets from his pockets. "Thought you lot could use some dinner. But if you don't want it, I'll just make my way back—"

"No, no, we want it," Gale said, cutting off Arthur.

"That's what I thought." Arthur handed a packet to Gale and another to Finn. "You can eat, right?"

"The bullet hit my hip, not my stomach, Arthur." The way Finn said Arthur's name made it sound like he really meant to say idiot. Gale suppressed a laugh at their brotherly bickering.

"Just wanted to make sure you aren't going to get sick," Arthur replied, and even in the dark of night, Gale could make out his rolling eyes.

"Of course, Mother," Finn said, rolling his eyes right back, or at least that's what Gale assumed.

Before he could get in between two squabbling brothers, Gale tucked into the dried meat and bread that Arthur had brought. Salt on the beef managed to suck up any remaining moisture that he had in his mouth. "Hey, Arthur, you got any water on you?" Gale asked, swallowing hard to suppress a cough.

"Sure thing, here you go," Arthur said, handing Gale a canteen. Gale took a couple gulps and then offered it to Finn. Finn grabbed it, hands shaky, clearly, despite his best attempts to seem fine, he was struggling. They needed to get him looked at by an actual doctor, sooner than later, Gale realized. Finn took a drink and handed it back to Arthur.

"So, what was with Sarge's yelling?" Gale asked.

"Well, we had to know where you lot were. S'not like Jagali is around this time to bring you two strays back," Arthur said with a strained laugh. "When he was yelling, I was starting to make my way out here. It was a distraction too, I suppose," he elaborated.

"Right, of course," Gale replied, that made a lot more sense to him. "Don't suppose he gave you the instructions he was yelling about?" Gale lowered his voice with the second question, knowing that it might perk up German soldier's ears.

Arthur nodded and leaned in and waited for the other two to do the same. When he was satisfied with how closely the three of them were, he started to speak. "The Indian Corps is going to make a move in the morning. We don't know when exactly, but when they do, they'll be charging the trenches." Arthur whispered so quietly that even though Gale was close enough to feel the other man's breath against his face, he could barely make out the words. It was clear that Arthur had the same concern about Gale, and didn't want them overheard by any German soldier who might be listening in.

"Right," Gale said.

"When they charge," Arthur continued, "We'll go in the opposite direction and make it back to the team behind the line."

"Sounds risky," Finn said, "I could barely make it here. Gale had to practically lift me up and carry me," he admitted.

Arthur hummed and nodded his head. He took a deep breath and looked up toward the night sky and then back at Finn. "Luckily, there are two of us that can help you make the trek."

Finn seemed hesitant to agree with that plan. "I don't want to be dead weight," he said after a beat.

"Too bad, you're going to be, and we're going to make it, right?" Arthur said, giving Gale a meaningful look.

"Yeah, like I said, I'm not leaving you behind. The Indians will give us the cover we need to make it back."

"And if they mistake us for a German?"

"They won't," Gale said quickly, doing his best to quell whatever angst was building in Finn's mind. Finn was prone to melancholia, and it simply wouldn't do for him to get that way now. "We just have to move forward, besides, our uniforms are totally different."

"Yeah we don't have the stupid little spike on the top," Arthur laughed.

"What is that even supposed to do?" Gale said, joining in. "Are they going to, what, head butt us to death?"

"Could you imagine? What, some general told them to use their heads, and the army took it seriously?" Arthur said between quiet laughs. Gale looked at Finn, who was shaking with silent laughter.

"Stop making me laugh, I'm going to reopen the wound," he protested.

"It'd have to be closed for that," Gale commented. The night continued on like that. Arthur and Gale traded jokes back and forth trying to keep Finn's spirits up. Eventually, exhaustion took over all of them and they managed to fall asleep. It was not the most comfortable night of Gale's life, but as the last dregs of adrenaline left his body,

Gale's body was forced to relax his muscles in a way that they hadn't done in months. Something about that night made Gale realize just how bleak things had seemed. It had felt like nothing had changed since January. They'd been fighting over maintaining the territory they already had and keeping the German's back. But it seemed like for once they were taking ground. The lines were moving. He was hesitant to get his hopes up that the war was going to end anytime soon. He knew it wouldn't. But as his eyes began to close for the final time that night, Gale felt like for once his optimism wasn't going to be misplaced. They were going to survive to fight another day. And when they did, they'd be that much closer to sending the Germans back home, tail between their legs.

CHAPTER 13

March 13th, 1915

The first thing that Gale was aware of was the shrieking sound of a whistle. After that, it was the overwhelming sound of gunfire. Then the sunlight that was doing its best to shine through his eyelids, forcing him to become aware. The smell of smoke and gunpowder burned his nose.

"MOVE!"

Gale suddenly became aware of the sergeant's voice cutting through the sound of the battle taking place above them. While it was barely a second in time between the time Gale started to wake and now as his eye flew open, his heart was already racing like he had been fighting for hours. Gale made eye contact with a man looking down at them in the mortar hole. It was a German soldier—this was what Sheppard was yelling about. Adrenaline pumped through him. Reflexively, Gale grabbed his rifle and pointed it at the German infantryman standing above them. He looked just as shocked as they felt. Perhaps he had assumed they were dead. As Gale pointed the gun at the German, he became aware of two things. First, his hands were coated in Finn's blood. He's sure that if he looked at himself, he was probably covered in it. Probably why the German must have thought they had all been dead. And second, that his rifle didn't have a single bullet loaded, not one in the magazine or even in the chamber. Gale elbowed Finn, knocking him into Arthur. The two brothers started awake, eyes wide as they looked at the soldier that Gale was holding at gunpoint. The two scrambled up into a more fully seated position.

The German mimicked Gale and pointed his rifle at him—the bayonet looked like it had just been sharpened. Gale thanked his lucky stars that the soldier looked younger than him and fresh-faced; he was probably too taken in by all that was going around him to be clear-headed. Before either of them could move, Arthur let out a guttural yell, pushed himself upright and tackled the German. The two struggle for a moment, but Arthur was not only bigger but also was clearly stronger. All it took was one well-placed punch and the young infantryman was down for the count. "I think that's our signal!" Arthur yelled, and he turned to wrap one arm around Finn.

There was fighting going on all around them. The German soldiers were covering No Man's land. It was going to be tough to make it through the fray unscathed. Gale quickly loaded his rifle. "That was empty?" Finn said, eyes wide.

"I was just as surprised as you are," Gale admitted.

"You are bloody daft, sometimes, aren't you?" Arthur commented, then said, "Ready?"

Gale nodded.

"Finn, you're going to need to brace yourself," Arthur said to his brother. "This is probably going to hurt a lot."

"Got it," Finn said. Arthur tightened his grip, and sure enough, Finn hissed in pain. "C'mon, let's go!"

The group climbed out of the mortar hole and began to move past the distracted soldiers. The Indian Corps was making its way onto the field. Gale watched as the two armies clashed. The Indian Corps fought valiantly, their barrage taking all of the focus off of Gale, Finn, and Arthur. The group made their way through No Man's land. They hunched over, Gale and Arthur stood on either side of Finn and supported him as they moved. Keeping low to the ground was the best option for them to survive the trek without becoming targets. As they moved, it became clear that the Indian Corps knew of their pres-ence, and they moved around them, easily and effectively. Despite the progress they made, it was getting harder to avoid German soldiers. The fighting was getting thicker and more violent, making it impossible to move without being caught. "We need to get to cover!" Gale yelled over the gunfire. It was getting too difficult to support Finn and to navigate the battlefield. The boys ducked into another mortar hole that was just in front of them.

"How are you doing, Finn?" Gale asked.

"Bloody fantastic," Finn griped.

"Got it," Gale replied. "We need to figure out what to do now. I can't see how we'll make it to our trench without getting shot at."

"Yeah, I don't fancy getting another bullet in me," Finn said, pulling up his shirt. At first Gale thought he was just trying to illustrate the point, but then he started to tug on the bandage, loosening it.

"What are you doing? We're in the middle of a battlefield, that's not the time to check on your injuries," Arthur admonished.

Finn rolled his eyes and began to re-secure the bandages. "I'm tightening them, they're slipping off, and I'd rather not lose the thing that's keeping my insides inside."

"Someone's testy today," Arthur snarked.

"I think I've earned the right—"

"Guys, we don't have time for an argument! Get it together, we need to figure out what comes next—" Gale started.

"What comes next is you come with me and my men." It was a familiar voice. Gale was getting tired of people walking up to their cover and interjecting. First Arthur, then the German, and now as he looked up, he saw it was Jagali. The captain was flanked by the same two riflemen that had been in the garrison with them. "We'll give you the cover you need to move, sound good, Privates?" he said, and despite it being a question, it was clear that Jagali wasn't asking at all.

"Yes, sir," Gale answered. Satisfied with the answer Jagali nodded at the two riflemen, and they moved around the mortar hole, and forming a wall, they held up their rifles and started to shoot.

The three boys got up. Gale and Arthur wrapped their arms around Finn's waist. Before they were good to leave, Jagali reached out his hand to Gale. Gale shook his hand. "You've done good. I heard what happened, very brave," he commented. "Your sergeant should be proud."

"Thanks, sir," Gale said. He released Jagali's hand and returned his focus to moving forward through No Man's land. There was so much smoke from the gunfire that a haze had settled over the field, making it difficult to tell where the trench was. But they had to move forward.

The three of them stumbled on, avoiding the barbed wire and shrapnel. They could only hope they didn't come across a mine. Arthur grunted and adjusted his hold on his brother. "Finn, I need to carry you," he said. "It'll be faster."

Finn looked around. "I—"

"Listen to your brother, Private, that's an order," It was the sergeant, he and Barry had found them in the fray!

"Sarge, glad to see your face, sir," Gale said, unsure what else could be said. A weight lifted off his shoulders that until that moment, Gale hadn't realized was there.

"Good to see you alive, Privates, we need to move out," Sheppard said. Gale turned to where he was looking and saw a group of German's managing to fight their way through a gap in the Indian Corps' line. Before Finn could try to protest again, Arthur hoisted his brother onto his back. Arthur was barely taller than Finn, so the middle McGuinness's feet almost hit the ground. In any other circumstance, it would have been a hilarious sight to see, but in that moment on the field, the pain etched into Finn's face and the determination on Arthur's wasn't anything but inspiring.

"Head on out, Private McGuinness. We'll cover you," Sheppard said. It struck Gale how similar Sheppard sounded to Jagali. They had the same sort of orders, same clipped tone. He was going to have to ask Sarge about how he knew Jagali soon. Now was not the time. Instead, joining Barry and the Sarge, Gale helped to form a small line shielding Arthur and Finn.

Gale lifted his rifle, looked down the ladder sight, and took aim at the team of Germans charging toward them. It was a bloody fight.

They were only able to take out a couple of the enemy soldiers before the combat turned to close range. Gale sliced and stabbed over and over again, barely taking the time to register what was happening. He used the forestock on the bottom of the barrel of the gun to block attacks. Some of the hits were hard, and Gale could only pray that the gun would break after repeated strikes. One German soldier moved into Gale's space, making it so the only thing he could do was block and dodge the slashing of the detached bayonet. Gale took a step back and lost his footing. He held his rifle up, using both hands so it was horizontal, the body of the rifle making a thin line of protection. Gale's heart pounded and blood rushed through his ears as time seemed to slow to a crawl. The German lifted up his own rifle, pointed it directly at Gale, and cocked the gun. Gale was frozen to the spot. He looked directly into the gray eyes of the German infantry man. If this man was going to kill him, he had to look Gale in the eyes. Then, before Gale could blink, the side of the German's head was blown out, bloody brain matter splattered everywhere, and the soldier's body collapsed to the ground like a marionette whose strings had been cut.

Gale looked over in the direction of the bullet that had shot the German to see Sheppard holding out his revolver, smoke still pouring out of the end of the barrel. "Thanks, sir!"

"Don't thank me, yet, we still have to get behind the line, now get up!" Sheppard replied.

Gale got up as quickly as he could, not wanting to lag anymore, especially since the sergeant had given him a direct order. He shoved a new magazine into his rifle and pulled the bolt. He aimed it at the last German soldier from the group that had charged at them. Barry was being outmaneuvered in the same way he had. He aimed, took a deep breath, checked the sight, and, as he exhaled, he squeezed the trigger. He felt the familiar recoil press into his shoulder as the bullet was propelled forward through the air, hurtling toward the German and hitting him square in the throat. Gale grimaced as the enemy soldier collapsed to the ground. The last thing he wanted to do was wound a soldier that badly and leave him to die a slow and agonizing death.

Barry looked at Gale and then back at the soldier. He said something to the German, but Gale was too far away to hear it. Then Barry lifted the rifle and pointed it at the collapsed infantryman. He pulled the trigger, and any struggle the German had left in him stopped. Barry must have felt the same way that Gale did about leaving a fellow soldier, even an enemy; to suffer on the battlefield long-term seemed unthinkable.

Barry turned to them, a grim expression on his face that Gale realized he hadn't seen before. He had dark circles under his eyes, and as Gale looked between him and the Sarge, he realized the two of them must have been up the entire night. Barry quickly made his way to Gale and the sergeant.

Sheppard looked at him and clapped him on the shoulder, which was the closest that Sheppard ever got to indicating he was proud on the battlefield. "Right, men, let's move." With that, the three of them jogged the rest of the way to the trench, each of them taking turns to look over their shoulders to make sure that there wasn't anyone following them. They finally made it to the trenches and jumped down into them. For the first time in two days, Gale felt himself exhale fully. He didn't have to be on high alert. There was no way for the enemy soldiers to make it all the way through No Man's land and into the trench. The artillery fire and gunfire were far too thick, as Gale had learned earlier.

"Sheppard!" Arthur yelled, grabbing the group's attention. He was still holding on to Finn, who, in the light of the day, looked more haggard than Gale had realized. The snark must have been his way of hiding the pain and exhaustion he was feeling. It may not have been that deep, but a bullet wound was always serious. Gale again hoped that infection hadn't set in yet.

They headed back through the trenches to the makeshift field hospital. It was really a dugout with a couple cots, two more gas lamps than the rest of the dugouts, and extra first-aid supplies. There was only one medic there when they arrived. *The rest must be on the field*, Gale realized. The medic quickly got Finn off of Arthur's shoulders and put him on a cot where he looked over Finn's injury. Much to

Gale's surprise, the medic that looked at the bandaging seemed satisfied with the job that Gale did. He re-dresses the wound, cleaning it out and sterilizing it. When the dried blood and dirt were washed away, Gale realized how red and angry the wound was. "It's not hot," the medic said. He had a strong Canadian accent.

"Right," the sarge said, "what does that mean for him?"

"Means there isn't an infection, yet. But he needs to be seen by actual doctors who can stitch him up and take out the bullet. Right now, it's fine, but if it were an inch over, we'd be having a different conversation. I don't want to risk moving it, just in case it does end up nicking something important."

Sheppard nodded. "Got it."

"He can stay here, then you and your team can go with him in the transport. You all look exhausted. Not the kind of soldiers that should be on the field," the medic said. Gale was shocked at how candid he was. But, it looked like he was a sergeant, too, an equal to Sheppard.

Sheppard nodded again, his lips set in a thin line. "Got it," he said again. He seemed frustrated yet was unwilling to press the issue any further. The medic seemed satisfied and moved on to the next injured lad that was being brought into the dugout. "We'll be right outside, Private, understand?" Sheppard said, gently, his hand on Finn's shoulder as he said it.

"Yes, sir, I'll be fine."

"Good, you aren't allowed to get any worse, not on my watch," Sheppard said, his face was grim and sincere, but his tone sounded like he was trying to joke or lighten the mood. It seemed to work; Finn managed to crack a smile.

"On it, sir."

With one more slightly awkward clap on Finn's shoulder, Sheppard and the rest of the team headed outside the dugout and waited.

And waited.

And waited some more.

The sound of the battle taking place just a dozen or so meters ahead of them sounded intense. There was yelling and screaming mixed with cannons and rifles shooting. Every once in a while there was an explosion that seemed to shake the ground. Mines were exploding underfoot. Gale could only hope that it wasn't anyone he knew stepping on them. He'd seen soldiers carried off the field with whole limbs missing from the mine's explosions. He dreaded the day that one would go off near him. *It wasn't a question of if it would happen*, Gale thought, *but when*. He just hoped he didn't step directly onto one.

Gale took off his helmet and ran his fingers through his hair, his fingers catching on the sweat-matted tangles in his locks. He raked them through, wondering when the next time he would get a chance to shower would be. He was covered in dirt, sweat, and Finn's blood. Gale decided not to think about the brain matter that was probably on him too from the soldier that Sheppard shot in front of him. Once he gave up on detangling his hair, Gale put his helmet back on, letting the leather strap dangle unlatched; he didn't have the energy or the care to properly put his helmet on.

Instead, he pulled out a cigarette and lit it.

"Haven't you inhaled enough smoke from the battlefield?" Sheppard asked.

Gale took a quick drag and shrugged. "What else are we supposed to do?" he asked. It was going to be a long wait until the sun fully set and the battle would be over for the night. Sheppard shrugged. Gale watched as Sheppard pulled out the pipe and filled it with some loose tobacco. As he packed the pipe, he reached out to Gale. "Give me your cigarette."

Gale handed it over and watched as Sheppard held the pipe between his teeth and lit the tobacco with Gale's cigarette. It was clearly something he had done many times before by the practiced way he handled both the pipe and cigarette. He quickly lit the pipe and took a couple of puffs before he ashed Gale's cigarette and handed it back. Gale took a drag and exhaled the smoke. He looked to Barry and Arthur, who had both pulled out their own cigarettes and were smoking. Gale's mother had always said that smoking was uncouth and a gross habit. She had lumped it in with chewing tobacco and public spitting. The practice was for people who were, in her words, down and out. Gale Sr. smoked a pipe and so did Gale's grandad, and Louisa didn't seem to have a problem with that. Her issue came with the hand-rolled cigarettes. "The tobacco will stain your hands and yellow your teeth. What girl will be interested in you if your teeth are the color of the Thames?" she had warned Gale when he was seventeen. Because of that comment, Gale had abstained from smoking for the most part. But now stained hands and teeth were the least of his problems. Dirt and blood were caked and crusted on his hands. Gunpowder had worked its way into his fingertips. The sharp, burning smell never fully washed out, no matter how much he tried. So he figured that the possibility of his fingertips getting an orange hue in addition to the black soot and dried blood that refused to leave his skin was no longer that big of a deal.

The team stood and smoked for a long time. The sun climbed into the sky and began to set. They were like sentries for the medical dugout. Soldiers passed them carrying their own wounded. Rushed medics ran in and out, collecting supplies and heading back to the battlefield. Finally, the sky began to darken, and the gunfire slowed to a stop. It was almost time for them to grab Finn and leave when a small group of Indian soldiers walked up to them, Jagali in the lead. It was strange to see Jagali off the battlefield, not only because it seemed like that's where the soldier seemed most at home but because the trenches were, in all but name, segregated. The Indian soldiers had their own section of the trench that they stuck to, probably because it was easier than dealing with the discriminating gazes of distrustful British soldiers. Loathe as Gale was to admit it, Sheppard's attitude to the Indian Corps was not uncommon, even if Sheppard seemed to have an alternative reason to dislike them than simple racism.

Jagali made eye contact with Gale and nodded. "Private Arlington, I'm glad to see you're still alive and well. How is the other?"

"Finn is fine, he's just laying down in there, sir," Gale said, nodding his head in the direction of the medical dugout. Jagali nodded.

"Good, I'm glad to see the three of you made it back. It would be a shame if the soldiers we rescued twice died on their way to the back of the lines." His voice sounded amused even if his face showed no evidence of him acknowledging the humor.

Sheppard's back seemed to straighten and his chest puffed out. It was subtle enough that if you weren't aware of his body language you might not notice the change. But it was enough that the team noticed and Gale was certain so did Jagali. The Indian captain turned to Sheppard. "May I speak to you privately, Sergeant?"

"Anything you have to say to me can be said in front of my men," Sheppard replied coolly. Jagali nodded his head, seeming unwilling to push the subject further.

"Well, I wanted to commend you, Sergeant Sheppard," Jagali started. Sheppard blinked a couple times, like he was trying to process the information, as if he couldn't quite believe what had been said. Jagali took a deep breath and continued, "We may have our differences, but your dedication to the men you lead is commendable. I have to say that I admire your willingness to be on the front lines right next to them. It's not that often that I see an English officer with those he commands." Jagali held out his hand.

Sheppard stared at the Captain's outstretched hand. For a moment, Gale thought that Sheppard was going to refuse to shake Jagali's hand. Then, Sheppard took Jagali's hand and shook it. "Thank you, sir, I appreciate the words."

Jagali nodded, then after a beat of silence, he turned to his men. "Right, we'll head out then. Godspeed men," he said, addressing the last phrase to Sheppard and his team before the Indian soldiers headed out. As they left, Sheppard seemed to deflate. He leaned against the wall of the dugout and took a deep inhale from his pipe. He held the smoke in his mouth and lungs for a beat until he finally exhaled.

"You good, Sarge?" Barry asked. He was always the type to not mince words.

"Just fine, Private," Sheppard said.

"You sure, that seemed tense," Gale added hesitantly.

"Yes, Private Arlington," Sheppard said. He took a deep breath and sighed, he looked resigned. "Captain Jagali and I know each other from back when I was stationed in India. We were assigned to the same patrol. We never got along. Things got worse when I ended up marrying the woman he had been engaged to," Sheppard said. "I hadn't realized things were arranged between them when I asked Leela's father for her hand, and no one told me until after the engagement was announced. There was a riot one day, and Jagali was supposed to be my partner. He shoved me into the crowd and abandoned me without a way to protect myself. My ribs got broken in the fray, and I was out for weeks because of him. Seeing him here ... just set me off." Sheppard elaborated, "But now, he seems to want to bury the hatchet. Don't think it'd be right to stop him from doing that, 'specially since he's made up for it by looking out for you lot." Sheppard took another drag from the pipe.

It was a lot of information to process. So Sheppard and Jagali did know each other. Not only that, but they had a past that seemed to be pulled from the sensational serials that were printed in the papers every week. Gale didn't know what to think. It explained why Sheppard had such a grudge against Jagali and the other Indian troops. Since Jagali seemed to be their main leader for the brigade that was stationed near them, Sheppard was hesitant that Jagali would let his old grudge take over how he treated Sheppard and his team. Gale was touched by how protective Sheppard really was of them. Especially since saving them was enough for him to count the grudge as settled.

"Christ, that's what the problem was?" Barry said, "I thought he had killed your best friend or something."

"Private Fritz, I'm advising you to tread lightly," Sheppard said, voice sharper than shrapnel.

"Yes, sir!" Barry said, quickly reminded of his place. He was probably worried that Sheppard would make him sprint back and forth in the trenches like he had when they were all in training.

Finally, the sun had finally set. Darkness ensconced the trenches and No Man's land. It was time for them to move out and get to the transport that was waiting to pull men out to rest and be treated by doctors. "We're heading back to Fiddler's Crossing and behind the line there," Sheppard said as they started the trek to the backline of trenches. Finn was back to being carried by Arthur.

"This is humiliating," Finn had said as Arthur hoisted him up.

"You can't walk fast enough, and we aren't missing the transport because of your misplaced pride, Private," Sheppard had replied. He was still in a strange mindset that Gale couldn't quite read, but he seemed to be lost in thought unless it came to barking orders at his men. Gale couldn't complain, he too wanted to get out of this trench and back to Fiddler's Crossing. It was the home he was longing for since he refused to think about returning to England. If he did that, he'd get too fixated on that idea and he'd be miserable. Instead, he thought about the well-insulated barracks they had managed to create in their dugout. He thought about how nice it was going to feel to be back in a place where he didn't have to think about whether or not his boots would be dry when he put them on. He wouldn't sink into the mud that made up the ground of No Man's land and the trenches they were currently in. He was confident that the Allies had made a great impact in the battle. From the way things were going, even the freshly rested German soldiers were struggling against their troops. Gale was optimistic that they would be able to hold the progress and soon make it to Neuve Chapelle. The small town was days away from being liberated from German occupation and a salient in the trench lines was going to bring a renewed energy to the troops. Gale was so certain that he knew that all he needed was a day's rest and he'd be ready to go out to battle again.

They wove their way through the complex maze that made up the trenches. It was difficult to know exactly where they were in the trench despite the labels that had been used to identify the different sections. Gale wished he had made a more detailed map. Or drawn one in his head. Instead, it was easier for them to just rely on their sense of direction. All they had to do was head westward in the trench and they'd eventually reach the back of the battle lines, and from there it would be easy for them to find the transport back to the Meuse and Fiddler's Crossing from there. Eventually they made it to the edge of the trenches and climbed out. Arthur put Finn down and waited for Gale and Sheppard to make it to the top of the trench, and they helped Finn get a leg up while the other two grabbed his arms and pulled him over the top. Barry took up the rear, making sure that they weren't going to get some last-minute missive that would say they had to stay longer. Gale stayed on edge until Finn was placed in an ambulance filled with many other wounded soldiers. Soon after, they headed to one of the transport trucks. Gale leaned his head back, letting the metal bar that made up the skeleton for the canvas covering support him. He took one last look around the truck, surveying his team, and felt comfortable knowing they were all there and that Finn was going to be in good hands.

CHAPTER 14

March 14th, 1915

The transport back to Fiddler's Crossing was unremarkable. It was so unremarkable that it had become remarkable. It was the first time in weeks that Gale hadn't thought about the stresses of the battlefield. Rather, he was able to take stock of himself. He clenched and unclenched muscles, making sure they didn't have any cuts or open wounds he had missed over the last few days. Gale was relieved to discover that he was, in fact, fine. He had a few bruises and the skin on his knuckles had split a little bit from being dried out and washing them over and over again in whatever water they had available to get clean at the moment. Once he was satisfied he hadn't magically missed a major injury, he pulled out his handkerchief. It wasn't the brilliant white that it was when he had first arrived on the front. Rather, it was now a dingy gray that showed evidence of it being repeatedly used, dunked in water and ringed out to get it as clean as he could with the limited soap they had. He wondered if he was going to see the mail carrier, Peter, again, so he could pass on a message to ask for a bar of soap from his parents. He knew he'd get a ribbing from the rest of the team about it, but he didn't care. He was getting tired of the permanently dirty feeling he had.

As it were, Gale took the handkerchief and poured some water on it from his recently refilled canteen. He used it to wipe off his face, neck, and hands. He scrubbed his skin over and over again, pouring water on to the handkerchief to rinse it as best as he could. The truck was trundling down an exceptionally bumpy road that made it difficult for him to be able to pour the water directly on the handkerchief. Rather it splattered around, pouring on the floor and through the slats of wood onto the earth below the moving vehicle.

"You're getting more water on the floorboards, you know," Arthur said tiredly from beside him.

"I know, I know. I just ...can't stand the feeling of dirt on my face anymore."

"You could just wait till we get back to Fiddler's Crossing and just bathe in the river," Arthur suggested.

Gale thought about it; it was probably a good idea, but the more he thought about it, the more he remembered the sight of the river after the first attack, before they dug in. There were bodies that littered the river. It was the place of the initial crossing—where the French and British pushed the Germans back. Soldiers from both sides lay decaying on both sides. The bodies had long since been cleared and buried or sent back home. But he couldn't get the images out of his mind. The idea of bathing in water that had been steeped by the dead was even less appealing than this riff on a sponge bath he was giving himself.

"I'll think about it," Gale said.

Arthur nodded, then he looked at Gale. "Did you know that all water is old water, Gale?"

"Uh, like the water cycle?" Gale asked, thinking back to primary school science.

"Yeah, all the water that we drink is the same water that was consumed by great leaders, cried out by centuries of people grieving endless lives that have been lost. It's the same water that was used to wash Christ's feet and to quench the armies of Alexander the Great as they pressed through the deserts to expand the empire. The same water that gets used to brew our afternoon tea is the same water that runs through that river. It's probably rained so much since the last time we were there that it's as clean as it was before any of us showed up. You know, eventually that's bound to happen ... I don't know. Finn said it better."

"Oh," Gale said, "how'd you know I was thinking that?"

"You turned green, Gale," Arthur said. He sounded like a tired parent. Gale wondered how long it had taken Arthur to perfect that specific tone. But he was the eldest brother, after all. "Look, I struggled with that too. It was hard for me to drink the water when we arrived because I was thinking the exact same thing," Arthur added after a moment.

"Oh, right, that makes sense," Gale replied. He hadn't really expected Arthur to struggle with that. He wasn't the most sentimental of the group, and therefore he was much better at compartmentalizing and rationalizing. He was like Charles that way. Nothing bothered them until they were alone with their thoughts. Perhaps the stress of his brother's injury and the long drive they had back to Fiddler's Crossing had given Arthur enough time to stew with his thoughts. Or the exhaustion that came along with being in battle for an extended period of time had finally taken a toll.

"You've also missed a lot of spots. But then again, I'm not sure they'd scrub out that easily," Arthur said.

"Oh, where?"

"Everywhere. There's something about the dirt that gets kicked up on a battlefield. It sinks into our pores, or something ..." Arthur mused, "never scrubs out the way normal dirt does."

"It's the blood," Sheppard said. His eyes were still closed, his head leaned forward, arms crossed. "It makes it stick more, cleaves it to your skin."

"Cleave? That's a word you don't hear often," Gale commented.

"My former commander was like a walking thesaurus. Guess it rubbed off," Sheppard explained, shrugging. Eyes still firmly closed.

"Of course he was, is there any kind of person you haven't met?" Barry said.

"I haven't met the kind of person who lets their sergeant get some shut-eye while in a transport," Sheppard replied. He rolled his shoulders back and leaned against the canvas cover.

Barry, Gale, and Arthur shared a look, quietly commiserating at the sergeant's unspoken order to be quiet. The rest of the ride continued on in silence. Gale dozed in and out of consciousness, letting himself be rocked by the bumpy roads.

When the truck finally stopped, Gale heard the familiar sound of the trench life during a relatively peaceful day. It was similar to the sound of the training camp they were at before they went to the first battle. Sergeants were yelling at privates to run faster, load their guns faster, aim better, hit harder. The usual. There was a cacophony of motors running as cars, trucks, and trains moved through the camp. The lurching of the truck signaling that it had shifted gears into neutral was enough to jostle Sheppard awake. He was immediately alert and standing. He headed directly out into the field. Gale and the rest of the team followed him out. They made a beeline to the hospital that was set up behind the trench. Finn was in surgery already; his truck had arrived twenty minutes prior. Gale cringed at the sound of men groaning and hissing in pain. Arthur decided to stick around, saying that he'd update them when Finn was out of surgery.

"You sure?" Gale asked, "I don't mind sticking around with you."

"I'm sure it's going to be a while, and I don't want Sheppard down another man. I promise you'll be the first to know, though."

Gale nodded and headed back to Fiddler's Crossing. They were told they were getting a week of rest before they'd get their next orders. Gale was thrilled. To make matters even better, Peter the mailman arrived. He gave Sheppard a large stack of what looked to be personal mail mixed with missives. Then he handed the rest of them a couple letters. The first one Gale looked at was a letter that could only have been written by Charles. He wanted nothing more than to tear into it and read about the adventures he and the rest of the Gallipoli boys were having. But, before he could, Peter settled down on the empty cot in their dugout.

"Say, where are the two McGuinness boys that went with you lot to Neuve Chapelle?" Peter asked.

"Field hospital," Sheppard said, eyes already scanning through the missives he was sent.

"Really, both got wounded?" Peter asked, concerned.

"Oh, no," Gale said, "Finn got shot, nothing too serious, but he's in surgery, and Arthur wanted to stick by his side. I think that's fair."

"Gotcha, how long do you think it'll be?"

"Couple hours until it's done, but who knows how long it'll take for him to get back on his feet," Barry guessed.

"Christ, I know you said it wasn't serious, but are you sure?"

"Yeah, I bandaged him up on the battlefield. It wasn't deep. I just didn't want to dig around for a bullet in No Man's land," Gale explained. As much as his fingers itched to read the letter from Charles and the rest of the team that was sent to the Ottoman Empire, it was nice to see a friendly face. Peter had gotten close to the team after Christmas, he often snuck them extra rations while they were being punished for the unauthorized ceasefire.

"Sounds like you all got up to quite a lot," Peter said. "Mind if you tell me about it while I rest my feet?"

"Sounds great," Gale agreed. The group got stuck in, listening to each other's stories, Peter told them about the influx of mail they had gotten recently. Apparently, Girl Guides and other charitable organizations started drives to make care packages for the troops. It seemed like the war lasting longer than Christmas, as was originally promised, had touched their countrymen.

"Why didn't we get a package?" Barry asked. "I could use some new socks," he added.

"You weren't here, that's why," Peter explained, "but next round I'll be sure to set some apart for you boys. It's not right that some parts of the trenches get the mail and others don't. The rest of the mail carriers and I are all trained for combat, no reason we couldn't meet you at the front."

Gale nodded, "Not sure it's worth it, I guess. I wonder if the commander thinks that we'd all be too distracted with thoughts of home to focus on the fight in front of us." It was a complete guess, but Gale wouldn't put it past high command to think that. He remembered his Grandad's warning about that thing. "The Crimean War would have gotten out of the way a lot faster if the brass had come down and taken a look at an actual battlefield, or better yet, just let the majors run things." It had been a common sentiment that was shared over and over by John and Gale Sr.

Now that Gale was at war himself and had met the very generals that they were talking about, he couldn't help but agree with them. They continued talking and Gale and Barry eventually invited Peter to stay in their dugout that night. Peter quickly agreed. "It's one of the better ones, if I do say so myself," he commented. Sheppard was still absorbed in the missives he had received. The more he read, the more furrowed his brows got. As the lads were about to head out to get dinner from the mess, Sheppard pulled Gale aside.

"Arlington, a word?"

"Yes sir," he replied. Barry and Peter lingered but Gale waved them on. He'd grab whatever gruel they had in a bit. Sheppard seemed particularly concerned, and he wanted to know why.

"Have you gotten any mail from Private Dunford?" Sheppard asked as soon as the other two were out of earshot.

"Yeah, I got a letter from him. I think it's got letters from Rory and Thomas as well in it."

"Mind bringing it over and reading it, quick?"

Gale was confused about what it was about but agreed nonetheless. He picked up the envelope with the familiar lazy scrawl that could only belong to one chap, Charles Dunford. Gale cleared his throat and tore open the envelope and began to read the letter. It looked like it was actually one long letter that was signed by all three of them.

"Read it out loud, please?" Gale was used to Sheppard's orders to do things, so the plea was unusual and set off an alarm bell in Gale's mind.

However, instead of saying anything, Gale took a deep breath and began to read. "Gale, hope this letter finds you in good health, et cetera, et cetera—"

"Word for word please."

"That's what it says, Charles is like that, sir," Gale explained.

Sheppard rolled his eyes, "Alright, then, continue."

Gale nodded and quickly picked up where he left off. "We have reached the coast of Gallipoli. The Aegean sea is bluer than I could ever imagine. Looking at the landscape it makes sense why there are so many myths from ancient Greece set here. It feels like a place where giants and monsters would fight. Feels fitting, since we're going to be taking on the leviathan of the Ottoman Empire. So far the most dangerous thing here is the sun. Rory is redder than a lobster. He spent the afternoon we landed playing footy with the Anzac boys and his skin had been blistered and peeling ever since! Seems like we're days away from getting into a battle with the Ottomans, and I for one am excited to do so, they need to be taken down a peg or two, just like the Huns."

Gale continued to read the letter aloud to Sheppard, each member of their team had their own sections. Rory spent half his time protesting he was as badly sunburned as Charles made him out to be. Thomas then re-confirmed that he was indeed very, very red. "He's so burned he can glow in the dark," Thomas described. It seemed to be great there, and Gale wished he was with them, in a truly foreign land, fighting the enemy with brothers who were exactly that in all the ways that mattered.

The more he read about how great Gallipoli seemed, the deeper the lines on Sheppard's face grew. Until finally Gale read the sign off. "Be sure to read this to the rest of the lads. We picked you because out of all of them, you'd be most likely to be the most sensical still. Send our best, Charles, Rory, and Thomas."

Sheppard let out a deep sigh that seemed to start at the base of his core and reverberate through the rest of him. He scrubbed his hands over his face.

"Arlington, I'm going to tell you something, but this cannot leave this dugout, understand?"

Gale quickly nodded—all he wanted was to be trusted by Sheppard.

"This is intel that I got from an old friend. I wrote to him knowing he was being moved out to the Middle Eastern campaign. I told him some of my men were going over. He sent a telegram to me.

I'm not supposed to know this, and you certainly shouldn't even be aware. But ..." Sheppard trailed off like he didn't know what he was supposed to say next. Gale wanted to shake him, to tell him to get to the point. He knew that whatever Sheppard was going to say was going to be bad. His mind quickly started to consider all the worst-case scenarios.

"Sir?" he asked, trying to prompt the sergeant to elaborate.

Sheppard looked at Gale like he was sizing him up. "I mean it, not a word to anyone. Not even Arthur or Finn. Especially not them," he said.

At this point Gale's heart was pounding, what could Sheppard be about to tell him. Was Rory okay? Was Thomas? Charles? Gale nodded sincerely, not trusting himself to say the right words. Sheppard seemed to understand. He cleared his throat and ran a hand through his hair.

"The Gallipoli campaign ... It ... it's not looking good, Gale. Do you understand what that means?" Sheppard said.

Gale's already racing mind seemed to spin even faster. Sheppard couldn't be saying what he thought he was going to say.

"It's a disaster. Our men are getting massacred. Just as fast as the enemy, but still. It's ... we're not going to win it, and the people backing it back in the UK ... well, they aren't going to give up on it quickly, does that make sense?"

Gale nodded. His granddad's words ran through his mind once more. *If only the higher-ups could see the battlefield and realize that the boots on the ground are real, tangible men made of flesh and blood and aren't the damn tokens they push around on a map, war would be far less cruel.* Gale took a deep breath to calm down; he couldn't let himself spiral.

"What can we do, sir?" Gale asked.

"We wait," Sheppard said.

"Sir, you can't possibly be suggesting that, right?"

"I fear that's our only option. We have to sit on our hands and hope they send them back sooner than later. From the sound of the note, they'll be rotating soldiers out as much as possible to keep them fresh."

Gale wanted to march into the general's tent and demand that he get sent there. He felt sick thinking about how he had a week's reprieve from fighting and Charles, Thomas, and Rory were trapped on a peninsula, fighting to survive.

"I know you are upset," Sheppard started.

"Why did you have me read the letter first?"

"I wanted to know what they were seeing first. I needed to see how accurate the intel is."

"But the man who sent it to you, you trust him, right?" Gale asked, he desperately wanted to hear Sheppard say that he, the man who wrote him, was prone to dramatics. That a disaster really meant one battle hadn't gone well.

Sheppard sucked in air through his teeth. "I do, Gale, I'm worried about them."

"Why can't I tell the others about this?"

"You're made of tougher stuff. I know you can handle it. Arthur and Finn have a lot on their minds. Barry is ... he's a good soldier, but he'd be too affected by it. I know you're able to compartmentalize," Sheppard explained.

"But Arthur ..." Gale said, trailing off.

"You heard him in the truck, right? He's not normally like that. His mind is too filled with worry over one of his brothers. He doesn't need to worry about the other one too. You and I both know it."

Gale nodded, Sheppard was right. He understood what he was saying. Gale didn't know what he could say or do. He felt like he was spinning his wheels but was staying in place. He felt like one of the trucks when they got sucked in by the mud surrounding the trenches.

"Why don't you go and check in on them and see how Finn is doing, okay?" Sheppard suggested.

That seemed like a good idea, sure Arthur said he'd find them when Finn was done, but he knew that he wouldn't want to leave his brother. "Yes, sir." Gale started to head out.

"Oh, and Gale?" Sheppard called, pulling him from the trance

Gale had placed himself into. Gale turned and waited for Sheppard to say whatever it was that was weighing on his mind.

"I need you to promise me on your family's honor, that you won't tell them," Sheppard said.

"I promise, sir. Not a word," Gale said. Promising on his family's honor seemed like a lot, but then again, it showed just how serious Sheppard was taking it.

"Not a word," the sergeant echoed. "Dismissed, Arlington."

Gale took off through the labyrinthine trenches. He ran into Barry and Peter on the way through and invited them with him to check on Arthur and Finn. They stopped back at the mess, and Gale grabbed Arthur some rations, just to make sure he was actually going to eat something that night. Gale had a feeling if he didn't do that, Arthur would be too focused on playing sentry and watching over his brother that it didn't seem like he would remember that he had his own bodily functions to consider.

They made it to the field hospital. It was bustling with activity, nurses and doctors were running from one end to the other. Men were moaning in pain on almost every cot they had available. The smell of iodine and blood swirled through the air and filled Gale's nose. He tried not to gag as he thought about Finn's wound. He scanned the hospital until he saw Arthur's tell-tale stature. The trio made a beeline to the brothers. Gale's mind kept bringing up imagined scenes of Rory dying on the sandy beach of Gallipoli. Of massacred soldiers. Of Charles and Thomas being killed in combat. He wanted nothing more than to tell them about what he had heard from Sheppard, but he quickly stamped down on the impulse. Now was not the time. He promised the sarge he wouldn't do that.

"Hiya, Arthur," Gale said stiffly. Barry and Peter gave him a confused look, Gale never spoke like that. Gale was just glad that Arthur and Finn were too out of it to pick up on it too. Although perhaps they would have missed it anyway, after all, they had no idea that Sheppard had spoken to him.

"I'm awake too," Finn slurred.

"You alright, Finn?" Gale asked.

"I'm bloody wonderful," Finn said, words still eliding together, proof he was still under the influence of some strong painkillers.

"They gave him a lot of laudanum," Arthur said. "He's going to be loopy for the next few days, at least. Probably for the best, they gave him ten stitches for this guy," Arthur continued. He held up the bullet that had to have been embedded into Finn's hip. Looking at it, there was a small hole in it. It must have been damaged when the gunpowder exploded and the shell flew out.

"Makes sense now why it wasn't worse," Gale said. "That hole there slowed it down." Gale patted Finn's leg. "You are a lucky guy, you know that, right, McGuinness?"

"Luck of the Irish," Finn mumbled, then added. "Well, half Irish."

Gale laughed; only Finn would get caught up in technicalities while right after getting out of surgery and under the influence of laudanum.

"Can I see that?" Peter asked.

"Sure thing," Arthur said, handing the bullet over to Peter.

Peter reached into his back pocket and pulled out a small chain from a necklace. He threaded the chain through the hole in the bullet and held it up to Finn.

Finn's heavily dilated eyes followed the swinging movement of the bullet pendant. "Got this chain playing cards," Peter explained. He handed the bullet necklace back to Arthur. "You can wear that necklace when you get better, sound good?"

"That's great," Finn slurred heavily. The group laughed. The rest of the night progressed like that, the team and Peter laughing together in the hospital wing. It was almost enough to push any concern that Gale had about the Gallipoli boys. But every moment he thought he was going to forget for a moment, his mind conjured up ghastly images of his friends dead and sprawled across the beach, their blood mixing into the sand, being carried away by the Aegean waters.

Gale shook his head, he had to stop thinking about that. What mattered was who was in front of him at that moment. Finn was going to make it, and the team was stronger than ever, even with a couple men missing.

CHAPTER 15

April 15th-May 2nd, 1915

A little over a month had passed, and Gale and the rest of his team had been given an extended rest. The rest was well needed; Sheppard's team had been fighting non-stop for ages now, and so they were worn out. The day after they had arrived, all of them managed to sleep almost an entire twenty-four hours. All except for Sheppard and Arthur. Arthur stayed by Finn's side during his entire recovery until he was out of the hospital. He had brought his younger brother food every day and had helped the nurses tend to Finn. Arthur had said that it was because the medical personnel were stretched thin. Gale wondered if it's because he felt guilty that he hadn't been watching out for Finn. Gale couldn't help but feel guilty for a couple of reasons himself, not only had he still not told anyone about what Sheppard had told him about Gallipoli, but he should have covered Finn's back better. If he had done that, he could have pushed his friend out of the way of the bullet.

Sheppard had seemingly gone back and forth between the dugout and command. It was clear he was trying to get some sort of news about the Gallipoli and what their next assignment was, but everyone in the command tent was being tight-lipped. Or rather, Gale guessed they were being tight-lipped because of how frustrated Sheppard was when he returned to the dugout. He had taken to pacing the trenches at night as days had passed. He was clearly going stir crazy in a way that Gale completely understood. Sheppard didn't like sitting on his hands and waiting things out. In fact, he liked it even less than Gale did. Which, in all fairness, was quite a lot.

On the 22nd day of April, Gale was playing cards with Arthur, Barry, and Finn when Sheppard walked into the dugout carrying a wooden crate. He dropped it down in the middle of the circle that the boys had formed while they were playing. Barry looked like he was about to complain about Sheppard interrupting the round that he was about to win, but they all saw how serious Sheppard looked.

"We've received our newest orders, lads. We're heading to Ypres."

"Again?" Gale asked.

"Yes. They need as many reinforcements as possible. Things have gotten worse there," Sheppard said.

"How, sir?" Finn asked. He was doing much better now that he was out of the hospital, but the stray gunshots the British and German armies traded back and forth every once in a while seemed to make him jump more than they ever had. Gale wondered if he had some shell shock. He'd never ask; it would be rude. After all, the only soldiers that had that were the ones that got blown up, right? Not the ones that had gotten injured. Certainly not Gale, who still woke up dreaming about images of Michael bleeding out quickly on the ground all the way back in September of the previous year. Or from the imagined images of Charles, Rory, and Thomas dying in Turkey. Gale shook off that train of thought, he wasn't going to even consider it. Besides, he had only heard rumors of soldiers being shell shocked, he hadn't even seen it firsthand, so there was no proof such a thing existed, he rationalized.

"Open the crate," Sheppard said. Gale could have sworn he heard Barry mutter "Cryptic bastard" as he leaned forward and pulled off the top slats of wood from the crate. They weren't nailed in tightly, so it took very little time for Gale to break it down.

Inside the crate were five wax-covered canvas hoods with glass goggles where the eyes were meant to be and a tube fed down to a filter at the bottom. "What are these?" Gale asked.

"Gas masks, right?" Finn asked.

Sheppard nodded.

"I heard about them when I was in the field hospital. The Germans have started using chemicals to create a gas that gets carried over No Man's land. They drop it from planes over the trenches," Finn's voice sounded haunted. "I saw a man covered in blisters that had been brought in from Ypres. The doctor was surprised he was still alive. He could barely breathe. Guess his lungs were burned too. Whatever the gas is ... it's really bad."

"You're right, McGuinness. Which is all the more reason we need to head out and help our fellow soldiers. We're refreshed, we're ready. All we need to do is train up on the gas protocols and we'll be ready to join them."

Finn swallowed heavily. Arthur put his hand on his brother's shoulder. That action seemed to ground the middle McGuinness brother. Each of them grabbed a gas mask. They were heavier than Gale had expected. Rubber and metal formed the seal around the breathing apparatus and the goggles. He didn't want to imagine putting it on. He had a feeling it would feel almost as suffocating as the gas, surely.

"Do we know what kind of gas?" Gale asked.

"Chlorine."

"What, like in pools?"

"That exactly," Sheppard said. Gale thought about the way his eyes would burn if he opened his eyes in a swimming pool. How the stench of it made his nose smart when he went to watch Charles in a swim meet. He thought about how it stripped Charles' already blond hair of color, making it even lighter. The concentration of the gas must be really high. It had to have been as bad or even worse than what Finn had described. After all, the soldier in the hospital was alive and he was lucky to be covered in blisters. The likelihood of other soldiers being dead was much *much* higher. A chill ran down his spine. The team focused as Sheppard explained all the protocols for a Gas attack. He talked about how sirens would warn them. Even though it was hard to dodge the gas, it was a sickly yellow color. It would float over No Man's land and be easily visible. They'd have more than enough time to put their gas masks on. They were told that chlorine gas was water-soluble, and they were to drench their clothes if they thought they were contaminated by it. The faster they could do that the better. They drilled the different techniques until Sheppard was satisfied. Then, he drilled them again. It was just like basic. It took a little over a week for Sheppard to be happy with their training. Or as happy as he was going to be when it came to their training. It was time to ship out.

In Gale's mind, the beginning of May brought the excitement of late spring hinting that the beginning of summer. When they arrived at Ypres, all thoughts of warm sun and brilliant green grass and flowers, and pretty girls were driven from his mind. The scene in the trench as they unloaded from their transport was desolate. Everything was dead. There were no trees with vibrant leaves and buds, the grass was long dead and yellowed, trampled into earth. It was eerily quiet, like not a single soldier was willing to say anything. They descended into the trench where they met Sergeant Wallen, a tall, wiry fellow whose eyes held a far-off gaze that Gale had never seen before in another living man.

"Welcome to hell, Gentlemen," Sergeant Wallen said. "Things have been getting worse, therefore your reinforcement is greatly appreciated," he added as he clocked the dubious looks Sheppard and the rest of the team had given each other. He led them through the trench, and Gale was astonished at the sight he saw. There were decaying bodies tossed over the parapets. Soldiers that had the hollow look that Wallen had, blankly manning the machine guns. The stench of rot mixed with sharp chlorine wafted through the air. The breeze rattled hauntingly through the trees, their branches clacking together as if it were late autumn and not in fact spring.

Gale looked down when he heard wordless chattering. Sitting on the edge of a dugout was a private that was rocking back and forth, picking at his eyelashes. With a second look, Gale realized that he had already plucked out his eyebrows. Gale had to turn away, only to see a group of soldiers wearing their gas masks tucked into their jackets.

The masks made them look like strange, inhuman creatures. Gale couldn't even make their eyes out through the glass of the tinted goggles.

"You're going to want to make sure you always have your masks with you, we get at least one attack a day, sometimes more," Wallen said, then he turned around. "Right, this is your sector. Here is your dugout and here is your machine gun. Make sure they don't advance. Good luck to you all."

Without another word, Wallen left. The team looked around the area they were given to man just as another breeze blew ominously through the trench. Gale wondered if every breeze that came through would make him worry about a gas attack. Something told him it would.

"Hey, Sarge?" Barry called by the machine gun. "Do we have anything to clean a gun with?"

Gale turned to see what Barry was talking about, only to see that the machine gun and the lookout positions were covered in blood and gore. It looked old and brown. He turned to look into the dugout the same time as a large rat ran out of it.

"We're not going to be here long boys, I promise," Sheppard said, but his face was giving away the lie he was telling. *Welcome to hell was apt*, Gale thought. This wasn't what war was meant to be. It was meant to be honorable. Not a graveyard. It was supposed to be men fighting for their beliefs, not driven crazy by chemicals that floated through the air and suffocated people to death. As Gale stood in the trench looking at the desolate surroundings, he realized that this must be what it is like to lay in a grave. A shiver ran down his back with another unwelcome breeze. He could only hope that they weren't going to be in Ypres too long.

End of Book One.